Gian

The Commonwealth of Israel

God's Eternal Purpose Unveiled

The Commonwealth of Israel – God's Eternal Purpose Unveiled

By Gian Luca Morotti

Foreword by: Dr. Gavin Finley

ISBN: 979-8-9855176-2-0

Printed in the United States of America
Publication House: Commonwealth of Israel Foundation
info@commonwealthofisrael.org or https://commonwealthofisrael.com/
Phoenix, AZ
In Cooperation with:
Douglas W. Krieger, Editor-in-Chief - Tribnet Publications, Sacramento, CA
https://www.facebook.com/TribnetPublications/
Cover Design by Stella Brookes, UK Artist, 2024

Ordering Information: Special discounts are available on quantity purchases by corporations, associations, educators, and others. Contact the publisher or distributor for details: info@commonwealthofisrael.org
Commonwealth of Israel Foundation – P.O. Box 31007, Phoenix, AZ 85046
U.S. trade bookstores and wholesalers: Please contact the distributor.

COMMONWEALTH OF ISRAEL

God's Eternal Purpose Unveiled

By
Gian Luca Morotti

Foreword by Dr. Gavin Finley

Commonwealth of Israel Foundation

PHOENIX, ARIZONA

Table of Contents

Dedication

To those who are on a pathway of discovering the ways of God and who have always had before their eyes the vision of His multi-faceted wisdom. May they now find another confirmation of it in this writing as well.

Acknowledgements

I could not have undertaken this journey without being inspired by the pioneers in the study of this most important topic of *Commonwealth Theology* (or *Grafting Theology*), among which, are my colleagues at The Commonwealth of Israel Foundation, to whom I would like to express all my deepest appreciation. A special thanks to Doug Krieger, the editor, for encouraging me in this project whereby my contentions were strengthened making my thesis even more convincing, radiating God's truth within these most critical matters.

Endorsements

Chris W. Steinle – *The Commonwealth of Israel – God's Eternal Purpose Unveiled* - provides a concise digest for those pursuing the biblical relationship between Christians and Jews. Gian Luca "sets the record straight," affirming that the "elect from among the nations" are brought into the "Commonwealth of Israel"—not separated from them. Morotti explains how the Christian's fellowship is as much with the Old Testament saints as it is with believers today. This agrees perfectly with Hebrews 11:39-40, "*And all these, having obtained a good testimony through faith, did not receive the promise, God having provided something better for us, that they should not be made perfect apart from us.*" We have in fact, been perfected together by the blood of the cross. — C. W. Steinle, author and charter member of The Commonwealth of Israel Foundation.

Ed Doss - The quest for personal restoration and spiritual unity amongst those who profess faith in Christ has been a pervasive aspiration throughout the ages. However, for many, these aspirations remain elusive and are often dismissed as fanciful musings of the gullible. Gianluca's work deftly navigates this complex terrain by elucidating the scriptural connections that undergird our faith(s), thereby facilitating a comprehensive understanding of the Father's eternal objectives. This book represents a seminal contribution to the discourse on spiritual restoration and the true unity of the *ekklesia*, providing readers with a lucid exposition of the divine plan to bring these objectives to fruition. The reader only needs ears to hear and eyes to see. – Ed Doss is founder of the on-line teaching group: "Digging Deeper" in Dallas, TX. BoD, The Commonwealth of Israel Foundation.

Peter Tsukahira - Gian Luca Morotti has written a thoughtful, well researched and very readable book! Through it I have been introduced to Commonwealth Theology and have begun to appreciate its contribution towards the wholeness of Yeshua's magnificent end time's bride. *The Commonwealth of Israel - God's Eternal Purpose Unveiled* will be helpful in bringing Gentile Christians closer to their Hebraic and biblical roots and strengthening their faith in the God of Israel. Peter Tsukahira is the Co-Founding Pastor of Carmel Congregation (Haifa, Israel).

Dr. Douglas Hamp - For those who have been wondering why some of the theological puzzle pieces don't seem to fit, this book provides the answers! This is a must-read for all who desire concise and scriptural answers to God's Eternal Purpose. – Dr. Douglas Hamp, Sr. Pastor, The Way Congregation, Denver, Colorado, USA.

Chuck Reber — Gian Luca's book, *The Commonwealth of Israel - God's Eternal Purpose Unveiled*, is treasure trove of biblical truth and revelation concerning Paul's mystery concerning the Gentiles and Jews being joined together in the Commonwealth of Israel. This book is for the Berean disciples, who " . . . received the word with all eagerness, examining the Scriptures daily to see if these things were so" (Acts 17:11 ESV). I really appreciate the way Gian Luca continually uses Scripture to interpret Scripture as he lays a solid biblical hermeneutic for Commonwealth Theology. The author weaves a beautiful tapestry of the grace of God by using texts from the historical books, the Psalms, the prophets, and the gospels, to show how they come together to reveal God's eternal purpose for the One New Man in the Commonwealth of Israel. In my 40+ years of pastoral ministry, and the dozens of books I've read on the subject of the church and Israel, I can't think of a book that spells out a clearer, rock-solid biblical case for this glorious truth. – Chuck Reber, retired pastor and founder-director of Prepare The Way Today Ministry: A Biblical Perspective on Preparedness and Crisis.

Scott Harwell - When Yeshua prayed for His disciples to "Be One," this not only applied to them as individuals but in spreading the initial and only gospel of the restored kingdom of Israel. Sadly, THIS gospel of the kingdom was not proclaimed for approximately 1700+ years due to Roman influence which essentially created a new religion. It is not a coincidence that the author and many others are now seeing what it means to be in covenant with the God of Israel. Upon entering covenant, we were ALL former pagans/heathens/gentiles who WERE EXCLUDED as citizens of Israel. However, NOW we are no longer strangers and aliens but are fellow citizens with the Holy One. This realization of our true identity and citizenship is growing exponentially as we are witnessing the dry bones put on sinews and the birth of a nation as it returns to His Way and Truth. Deuteronomy 4 and 30 are still in the embryonic stage but it is happening. When Messiah returns, THEN and only then will the jealousy of Judah/Judaism and Ephraim/Christianity be completely vanquished. There will then be only one house and one nation. This book by my brother will help you discover your citizenship and how to be an ambassador for the Kingdom in spreading the Truth and the Way to both our Jewish and Christian brothers and sisters. – Scott Harwell, Esq., BoD, The Commonwealth of Israel Foundation.

Foreword

Anesthesiology is a demanding discipline. For 35 years that was my world. In the operating room serious medical and surgical issues could arise suddenly. And they often did. Sometimes the issue was deeper and more complex than seemed apparent at the time—often it was life-threatening. A root cause analysis was essential to get to the heart of the problem. An accurate diagnosis was needed; and quickly, to get things turned around.

Among many in the evangelical community there is a growing concern. Why is our Western church in such moral decline? Faithful Bible study into the restoration at the end of the age is sorely neglected. So, where is the much-lauded Berean diligence? Are we not called to search the scriptures? Where is the intel? Where is the spiritual preparation? How is the story of this age going to end? And are we spiritually ready to face the challenges up ahead? It was out of this awareness, and as a result of personal challenges, that in 2000 AD I set about creating the website, EndTimePilgrim.org. This was followed 7 years later by my YouTube channel.[1]

I have always found inspiration in the accounts of explorers and surveyors. These pathfinders blaze the trails, opening the way ahead for those who follow. Followers of Messiah are in a similar mode. The end-time scriptures need to be explored. The main issues need to be identified. Eschatology calls for biblical cartographers to map out the future 70th Week, (or 70th Seven), of Daniel, and the final seven years of this age. This is the final section of the timeline for the period God said He has "determined" or "set apart" in the Seventy Weeks prophecy.

[1] https://www.youtube.com/user/gavinfinley

The end of the age is where the Holy One of Israel will attend to His unfinished business. He will take His covenant people "back to the future," returning them to the ancient paths. Seemingly conflicting pieces of the puzzle sit there on the table. They are destined to come together in beautiful harmony. This includes that missing section of theology that we might call *Israelology*.

The Fall Feasts of Israel[2] need to be examined, and evaluated beyond the lenses of rabbinical tradition, or HRM[3] religious reasonings. They appear to connect into the final seven years of this age, and very precisely so. These festivals are eternal. This calls for a deep and serious study into their spirit, character, and end-time purpose. In future years these special autumn dates located on the Hebrew calendar are and will be fulfilled in the New Covenant. These Fall Feasts are divine appointments. They will erupt into holy history in a very spectacular fashion.

So, what will be going on in that future end-time drama? Why did Moses give that message to us in Deuteronomy 4:23-31, and in the Song of Moses in Deut. 32? Why the reference to the "affliction of Joseph" in Amos 6:6? In the Olivet Discourse Jesus/Yeshua spoke of these latter-day trials of the saints. Are they necessary for the promised restoration to be achieved?

Most Bible teachers prefer not to address this. Biblical references to sifting and refinement can be disconcerting. Nevertheless, at the last page of the Book, we see that God wins. He brings the promised reconciliation of all things. The missing pieces of the puzzle will emerge

---

[2] http://endtimepilgrim.org/fallfeasts.htm

[3] HRM: The Hebrew Roots Movement has influenced hundreds of thousands of Christians in recent decades, and many more have encountered arguments from those in that group. The movement places a strong emphasis on Hebrew traditions and the Law of Moses. While many aspects of HRM have positively affected followers of Yeshua, other aspects have wrought growing controversy among Christians who have encountered its excesses.

out of the mystery to find their place. The prophet Daniel concluded, "*The wise will understand*" (Dan. 9:10).

It has been my privilege to have known and to have co-written books with a handful of faithful men and women. They are given to diligent study in biblical truth in the love of Messiah. They have a certain zeal to understand the divine purpose, and to press in to discover what the Holy One of Israel has planned. In 2019 we gathered at the third annual One in Messiah Convocation in Denver, Colorado. The book, *One in Messiah*[4], is a compendium of 12 authors out of nearly 20 participants who collaborated that year. Out of that came the *Denver Declaration*[5] which lays out the inspiring new doctrinal themes of the Congregation/Commonwealth of Israel. That was followed soon after by the book, *Commonwealth Theology Essentials*.[6]

Among this growing company of biblical students and devotional writers is our Italian colleague, and dear friend, Gian Luca Morotti. He is a Hebrew scholar who now lives in Italy. It was in late 2020 that I read his first book, *Called to a Holy Pilgrimage, the Gathering and Restoration of the House of Jacob*.[7] I was greatly impressed with his biblical scholarship, and the way he applied this to our devotion to Messiah. His keen spiritual insights into the restoration of Israel are extraordinary. I had the privilege of interviewing him and discussing his book in a 12-part series on my

[4] *One in Messiah – Perspectives on Commonwealth Theology Presented at the Denver Convocation 2019* - https://www.amazon.com/One-Messiah-Perspectives-Commonwealth-Convocation/dp/1073399702

[5] *The Denver Declaration with Bible References* - https://www.amazon.com/Denver-Declaration-Bible-References/dp/1687372144

[6] *Commonwealth Theology Essentials* - https://www.amazon.com/Commonwealth-Theology-Essentials-Douglas-Krieger-ebook/dp/B088X3ZJBR

[7] *Called to a Holy Pilgrimage, the Gathering and Restoration of the House of Jacob* - https://www.amazon.com/Called-Holy-Pilgrimage-Gathering-Salvation/dp/B08LQRVJQB - Gina Luca Morotti

YouTube Channel. He brought out the numerous biblical passages pointing to the ultimate restoration. These included the two olive trees of Zechariah 4, the two sticks of Ezekiel 37, the reunion of the two houses of Israel, and the raising up of the Tabernacle of David in Judah. These have implications for the uniting of Judah, Ephraim, and the "remnant of mankind" (Edom/Esau), even gathered from all the nations, under the banner of the United Kingdom of David (Acts 15:16-17; Amos 9:11-12). Gian Luca outlined a future joint operation of the two houses (Judah and Joseph) serving Messiah as "One New Man," thereby establishing the full restoration of what the apostle Paul calls: "*All Israel*" (Rom. 11:26).

Those who take responsibility for the future 70th Week of Daniel often come to a common conclusion. Our present Western theologies of Israel and the end-time are seriously flawed. For the past 175 years Dispensational theology[8] has been dominant among Western evangelicals. This theology is problematical. It has dispersed the Church and Jewish Israel into separate theological boxes. It has assigned separate divine purposes and separate destinies to each of the estranged parties. There is no expectation of any reconciliation between the two. Does the Almighty have a plan for the Church and a separate plan for Israel?

This "apartheid of the Elect" or "ghettoizing" of the Jewish house, is unfortunate. It continues to ratify the Constantinian accord which sidelines and alienates the royal Jewish house. Dispensational theology also leads us on to a strange conclusion, one which is quite alien to the scriptures. Dispensational theology sees two *elects*, and two separate eternal destinies for two companies of chosen people. Is our Messiah, (the Bridegroom in biblical typology), returning to marry two brides—one, the

[8] Please review the scope of Dispensationalism found @ https://en.wikipedia.org/wiki/Dispensationalism

Bride of Christ for New Testament saints and the other, the Wife of Jehovah, for Old Testament saints?

Reformist Christians have correctly affirmed that there is just one covenant (viz. the New Covenant). However, they generally see no vital Jewish involvement in the end-time ingathering, and certainly no distinction between Judah-Israel and Ephraim-Israel. But as we see in Ezekiel 37 the Jewish stick of Judah will be joining the stick of Joseph, (which had been in the hand of Ephraim). The two will be put together and placed into Messiah's hand to become one stick.

Few in Reformist circles seem to appreciate this. Many are discounting any future gathering of Judah (Jewish people) to their ancient homeland, considering this to be unbiblical or certainly physically impossible.[9] Nor have many of them come to understand that the promised end-time Jewish redemption of Zechariah 12 will surely come, and how it will be such a blessing for all of us. So, they continue to follow the same Replacement Theology as the Church of Rome. These flawed theologies are of serious concern. They can, and they have, fed into evil political movements, spawning grievous histories, even Inquisitions, Pogroms, and the Holocaust.

So, what was it that split Israel into two kingdoms? Why did the ten tribes rebel against the Jewish House of David? In his text Gian Luca

---

[9] Louis Berkhof, a leading amillennialist (Reform theologian) in 1938 (the very year of Hitler's "Kristallnact," the "Night of Broken Glass," which sealed the doom of over six million Jews throughout Europe wrote this in his *Systematic Theology* (Grand Rapids, MI: Eerdmans, 1974, p. 712): "Premillennialists . . . maintain that there will be a national restoration . . . of Israel, that the Jewish nation will be re-established in the Holy Land—and that this will take place immediately preceding or during the millennial reign of Jesus Christ. It is very doubtful, however, that Scripture warrants the *expectation that Israel will finally be re-established as a nation* . . .." (italics mine). (Ref. Douglas R. Shearer's text: *Amillennialism, Theology or Metaphysics*, self-published, p. 22)

Morotti examines the "Breach of Jeroboam." He points to the law vs. grace issue, at the heart of the furor. This tug-of-war over these God-ordained priorities caused the schism between the royal Jewish house of Israel (Judah) and the ten tribes that became the Northern Kingdom. After the Assyrian captivity, that wild, scattered ten tribes eventually re-emerged, crystallizing in the nations primarily in Western Christendom.

This "family feud" continues to this day. The cause of the rebellion is explained in this book. With this understanding we begin to see the clue to the repairing of the breach, which comes through the person and work of the indwelling Messiah. The reconciliation between the two feuding companies is a prophesied future certainty uniting the Congregation with the Kingdom. The jealousy and the mutual vexation will end. This union is firmly established in the New Covenant, through the atoning blood of Christ. This is laid out by our apostle Paul in Ephesians 2:11-15. The matter of citizenship in the Kingdom of Messiah is also an unrealized blessing. This new realization of our identity in Israel's Messiah is a true peacemaker, and especially so as we enter the national sovereignty crises of the latter days. This latter-day Yom Teruah (aka Feast of Trumpets) call of allegiance to the Kingdom of Messiah is a hidden future reality, and a Kingdom sovereignty issue of great international importance, truly awesome in its implications. Very few Bible prophecy teachers have dared to address this.

The prophetic passages are clear. There is to be a future, unprecedented reconciliation in Messiah (Ref. Ezekiel 37:15-28). Both houses are to be re-united, and with it the full restoration of All Israel. So what is going to happen in the witness of the last days? We also need to ask why these things must happen. If Messiah is to bring His beloved covenant people through the trials of the latter days, then what is His divine purpose in all this? Deep calls unto deep. We are then drawn to ponder this question. "What is our personal allegiance to Messiah, the King, and our corporate or group responsibility within His Kingdom?"

This matter happens to be precisely what Gian Luca Morotti is addressing in his new book, *God's Eternal Purpose; A Truth Restored.* This book, beautifully written in the European style, goes to the heart of God's agenda for the full restoration of all things. He addresses the vital issues of devotion in the end-time witness. He lays out the theological foundation for the prophesied reconciliation, the repairing of the Breach of Jeroboam, and the resolution of the 2,900-year-old family feud.

In Revelation chapter 7, we see the end-time Harvest ingathering. As stated by Daniel in Daniel 9:24, the transgression is to be finished. All vision and prophecy are to be sealed up for the Heavenly Court to be unsealed at the Judgment on the Last Day. Then finally, "*. . . to anoint the Most Holy Place*" whereupon the Messianic Age shall commence, and the Anointed One shall take His rightful throne. As we read in scripture, "*David My servant shall be king over them, and they shall all have one shepherd*" (Dan. 9:24; Ezek. 37:24).

Gian Luca featured this Harvest theme in the graphic picturing the sheaves. We remember Joseph's dream, and the persecution he suffered at the hands of his brothers. In this same *Joseph anointing* God's covenant people will again be ministering the *Increase*, and gloriously so, during another seven-year time of famine. This time it will not be a famine of bread, but "*a famine of the hearing of the Word of God*" (Amos 8:11).

But the Holy Spirit outpouring found in Joel 2:28-32 will be there. Yes, the Latter Rain will prophetically unfold to bring in the End-Time Revival, ripen spiritual seed to fruition, and bring in the Harvest. The sheaves of all 11 brothers of Joseph will be there as well, bowing down before the sheave of Joseph. As we see promised in Isaiah 49:6, all 12 tribes are fully involved in this plentiful end-time ingathering.

The Servant Israel, (the Body of Christ united to Christ the Head), will be a Light to the Gentiles, to bring the salvation ordained by the Father to the ends of the earth, even right through to the end of the age.

In the Songs of Ascent there is much rejoicing as the tribes go up to the feasts in the Holy City of Jerusalem. Then at the end of the story, at the consummation, a remnant shall return.

Psalm 126:

He who sows in tears shall reap in joy. He who continually goes forth weeping, bearing seed for sowing, Shall doubtless come again with rejoicing, Bringing his sheaves with him.

So the restoration of both houses of Israel, the church (His Ekklesia) and Jewish national Israel (Judah), is fully assured. They are to be unified as a global Congregation/Commonwealth in Messiah. Both Moses and the apostle Peter speak of a cross-linked royal priesthood and a holy nation. The glorified saints are in all twelve tribes. The Elect will include people from every nation, race, tongue, and tribe. Messiah will gather all His jewels, as living stones, into a single spiritual house (2 Peter 2:5). Is not this God's Eternal Purpose—to "*head up all things in Messiah?*"

Surely, this is the ultimate glorious company spoken of in Hebrews 12:22-24 who " . . . *have come to Mount Zion and the city of the living God, the heavenly Jerusalem, to an innumerable company of angels, to the* ***general assembly and ekklesia of the firstborn****, who are registered in heaven, to God the Judge of all, to the spirits of just men made perfect, to Jesus the Mediator of the* ***New Covenant****, and to the blood of sprinkling that speaks better things than that of Abel.*" To say this is an eye opener, even a vision splendid, would be an understatement.

This is the full restoration of *All Israel* spoken of by the apostle Paul in Romans 11. In Revelation chapter 7 John in vision saw the end-of-the-age ingathering of all the saints before the throne of God. He saw people coming before the throne from all nations, a *melo-hagoyim* ("community" or "group" of "nations" or "multitude of nations" or "fullness of the Gentiles"), as numerous as the stars of heaven. All are one in Christ Jesus.

Our soon-returning Messiah is the One who reconciles and establishes this magnificent, promised unity. In the dual office of the Order of Melchizedek He is both our ministering High Priest and King of Salem/Prince of Peace.

There is a peace that this world longs for. It comes through the righteous rule of Messiah in the New Covenant. This is the only viable basis for world peace. This peace that passes all understanding begins in individual hearts. Then later, corporately and climactically, with His return in deliverance at Jerusalem. This is the only remedy for a world slipping into moral decline and international chaos. The end of the age will see Messiah "*put an end to sin*." The days of rebellion shall be "cut short," just in time to "save the planet."

So, our relationship to Messiah is more than membership in His Congregation. The Commonwealth of Israel is an extension of a national sovereignty, and a Kingdom drawing in people from all nations. In the New Covenant we see the conferring of citizenship, and a passport into the Kingdom of Messiah. The Second Coming will see Jesus' return as the Lion of Judah. He is the Shiloh (Prince of Peace), the one and only sovereign ruler to whom all Kingdom authority here on earth rightfully belongs---even "*My servant David shall be their Prince forever . . . Moreover I will make a covenant of peace with them*" (Judah and Joseph)—and "*it shall be an everlasting covenant with them*" (Ezek. 37:25-26).

Gian Luca Morotti, is surely at the forefront in advancing this understanding. He, together, with a growing number of harvesters are bound together in this calling. His book, *Commonwealth of Israel – God's Eternal Purpose Unveiled*, joins this gathering of biblically-based workers in God's harvest. It is a message of truth and inspiration for all the called, the chosen, and the faithful. For those who are drawn to the high calling in Yeshua, the Christ, this book is a treasure, and it comes with my highest recommendation.

May I leave you with this astonishing, all-inclusive, stereoscopic prophecy taken from Psalm 22:22 and Hebrews 2:11-13 saints throughout the ages:

So now Jesus and the ones he makes holy have the same Father.
That is why Jesus is not ashamed to call them his brothers and sisters.
For he said to God,
"I will proclaim your name to my brothers and sisters.
I will praise you among your assembled people (lit. *Ekklesia*)*,"*
He also said,
"I will put my trust in him," that is,
"I and the children God has given me."[10]

Blessings to all,

Gavin Finley MD

[10] Taken from the NLT: "Scripture quotations marked NLT are taken from the Holy Bible, New Living Translation, copyright (c) 1996, 2004, 2015 by Tyndale House Foundation. Used by permission of Tyndale House Publishers, Inc., Carol Stream, Illinois 60188. All rights reserved."

Prologue

When Paul wrote his letter to the Roman believers, he spoke of their "calling" in these terms: ". . . ***we are the called according to His purpose***" (Rom. 8:28).

God's eternal and unchangeable love and wisdom, demonstrated in redeeming a people for Himself unto holiness, from every nation, tribe, people and tongue, Who by the power of His will has chosen us before the foundation of the world and called us to be forever united as the collective Body of Messiah. This is the nexus of God's Eternal Purpose; wherefore, the Holy Spirit longs to reveal, expand and fix into our souls and spirits the full acceptance and membership in this very purpose.

In truth, He wants each one of us to come to appreciate their position in the ***household of God*** (Eph. 2:19), that is, in what the book of Hebrew calls ***His own house*** (Hebrews 3:6). This is nothing more than the family of God, both past, present and future—His actual polity, dispensation or administration on the earth today. He longs for you and I, as fellow citizens, to enjoy the riches of the Commonwealth of Israel (Eph. 2:12).

Yes, He wants you to know that all of this is already yours; it's yours by inheritance the moment you stepped into God's own family. Furthermore, He so much desires for you to be grounded in the biblically accurate design for restoring truths which were hidden in times past, but now revealed to us through the prophetic and apostolic Scriptures. These marvelous and unambiguous Scriptures point to the unity within His

Ekklesia (aka "church") the "one body" and "new man" and "new creation" being the culmination and the recipient of all His work of restoration. This is God's final instrument in fulfilling His eternal purpose. Having the keys of the Kingdom in its hands (Matthew 16:18-19), the Ekklesia, the assembly of the called out ones, is divinely energized, and equipped to the degree that it pursues that purpose.

I pray that you'll be filled with expectations to challenge yourself to know and practice this divine purpose and to contend for the ironclad truth on which everything rests: "*For by one Spirit we were all baptized* ***into one body*** *–whether Jews or Greeks, whether slaves or free–and have all been made to drink into* ***one Spirit***" (I Corinthians 13:10), to the glory of the Father, "*. . . till we all come to the unity of the faith and of the knowledge of the Son of God, to a perfect man, to the measure of the stature of the fullness of Christ*" (Eph. 4:13).

My prayer is that by reading this book your mind will be enlightened—yes, the "*eyes of your heart will be enlightened*" (Eph. 1:18) to the work of God, His plan and design for the ages.

This is what Scripture now openly presents to us as His Eternal Purpose, now being restored to its proper place in the Father's Household of Faith.

Chapter 1

God is in the Business of Restoration

Restoration, what a beautiful thing! Imagine finding yourself robbed and plundered, trapped in a circumstance where there's no way out; you feel like hidden in a prison house, helpless and deprived of your rights, looking for relief but not able to find a way out. Only the emergency response and intervention of someone from outside could put an end to this despairing, seemingly endless, situation you're in.

Also imagine that at the time of your deepest despair, when all hope is gone, someone comes your way and pronounces liberty over your life, proclaiming that the time of waiting has ended and that your cry for freedom has been heard. You hear words like: "*All the years spent in sorrow and agony have come to an end; you are now entering into a new season of joy and freedom never experienced before. You are restored!*"

How would you receive such a word that declares restoration into your situation? I don't know about you, but I would welcome such a release as coming from heaven itself. In reality true deliverance, freedom, and restoration can only be the work of God. Truly, God is in the business of restoration, but have you ever given a thought about God restoring a profound truth, which for various reasons has never before been fully grasped? Something that has always been embedded in your Bible to which you've scarcely given due prominence?

Would you have the same reaction if it were for a concealed truth? I refer to truths towards which whole portions of Christendom still struggle with because of past misconceptions or erroneous teachings and biases.

Let me begin by sharing with you a glaring example of what I want to say, in relating an episode that is portrayed in the book of the prophet Jeremiah at a time when Jerusalem had been given into the hands of the Chaldeans and into the hand of the king of Babylon, because of Judah's disobedience.

Due to the announcement of an impending captivity, those anticipating punishment hadn't the slightest notion of God's ability to restore both His "peculiar" land and nation/people. It looked virtually impossible; notwithstanding all the negative predictions and erroneous perception of things, some of the most positive prophecies about the future of the people of God are found in Jeremiah.

Jeremiah prophesied a restored nation with a new covenant with God[11]. And eventually, this happened. The Lord promised full

---

[11] David Pawson, Unlocking the Bible (Harper Collins 2015) p. 578

restoration of the people to their land and of the people to Himself through the means of what would be termed an ***everlasting covenant***. This everlasting covenant would forever call those under His judgment/punishment: ***My people*** (Jer. 32:38).

Nevertheless, in light of the plight in which they were living, there still were people that went on living in captivity with an attitude of bewilderment and despondency regarding this prophesied final fulfilment of God's promise of full restoration.

Albeit poignant, their prophetic destiny was so overwhelming that He kept speaking words of hope and comfort to the glory of His covenant faithfulness in the midst of their immediate plight and Fatherly discipline.

Thus, right when the taunt of the heathens and the scorn of other nations assailed—as they beheld what seemed to them the entire downfall of the two kingdoms of Judah and Israel—we find one of the most incredible promises of restoration found in Hebrew Scripture.

The repercussions of the would-be promise would impact the whole earth! So, in face of the allegation that He had rejected His two chosen families (viz., the House of Israel and the House of Judah), God forthright issues an amazing renewed confirmation.

Israel and Judah called the 'two houses of Israel' (Isaiah 8:14) or the two kingdoms of Israel and Judah would hear these divine pronouncements:

> "*Have you not considered what these people have spoken, saying, 'The two families which the LORD has chosen, He has also cast them off'? Thus they have despised My people as if they should no more be a nation before them*'" (Jeremiah 33:24).

> There is an inherent promise to the House of Judah and the House of Israel, domiciled within the ***new covenant*** concerning the "two families which the LORD has chosen." They, Israel and Judah, once separated by intense hatred for each other, would once again be REUNITED as His UNITED Kingdom!

On the full manifestation and fruition of this ancient prediction I have dedicated the remaining chapters of this book. For now, it is enough to focus on the fact that in the Lord's eyes Israel and Judah were just ONE NATION. Despite the separation between the two kingdoms (Judah and Israel—2 Chron. 10-11), God saw them united once again. YHVH reveals, the LORD is by nature, the God who brings things to full restoration unto the day He fulfills all His promises. This is evidenced by a message that still resounds from the pages of the New Testament when Peter, enlightened by the Holy Spirit, was able to voice a life-changing and prophetic message:

> "*Therefore repent and return, so that your sins may be wiped away, in order that times of refreshing may come from the presence of the Lord; and that He may send Jesus, the Christ appointed for you, whom heaven must receive until the* ***period of restoration*** *of all things, about which God spoke by the mouths of His holy prophets from ancient times*" (Acts 3:19-21 NASB).

In Peter's foretelling message, a time would come when a great restoration would signal the end of days. I believe that the time we are living in sees us at the center of this process of restoration that will end and be perfected with the coming of the Messiah, the Deliverer (Rom. 11:25-27).

As we're entering the very last phase of human history, the apostolic calling to repentance weighs on us even more—upon whom the end of the ages has come[12], and as a burning lamp diffuses the warm light of a prescient word for this generation. Notwithstanding, are you willing to cooperate with the Holy Spirit in God's restoration? Read on and see why it's in your very best interest.

In the above verses, the Greek word for ***restoration*** (*ἀποκαταστάσεως*) stands for *restitution* or *reestablishment*[13], that comes

[12] I Corinthians 10:11

[13] (Strong's Concordance #G605)

from the verb *apokathistemi*, meaning *reconstitution*. Moreover, the expression ***of all things***[14] denotes the whole, of every kind, including all the forms of declension. In other words, the apostle Peter is as if he were saying that the end-times would be characterized by a great movement of reconstruction of all the forms of deterioration. If we compare the Hebrew New Testament, it expresses a similar idea of everything returning corrected, amended, and repaired[15].

Most assuredly, God is up to something. His desire in this generation is to reignite and restore the truth of His eternal purpose which is to return us to a massive course correction prior to the second coming of the Lord Jesus.

And yet if we look at history, we'll have to admit that not all things were always as clear as today. Yet God is in the business of restoring His ultimate intent. We need to understand that He has always had a plan to first incorporate things previously revealed into pieces of multiple generations into one ongoing expression of purpose here on earth. In fact, when these truths become part of our spiritual inheritance, revealing what God is calling us into, then we

---

[14] (πάντων - Strong's Concordance #G3956)

[15] Acts 3:21, *Modern Hebrew New Testament*, 1995, The Bible Society in Israel

are ready to receive His ultimate new restored truth by the agency of the Holy Spirit guidance and teaching[16].

In his book, *The Days of the Saints*, Dr. Bill Hamon defines the expression *restoration movement* arguing that it is used by Church historians and theologians to describe a time when the Holy Spirit acts sovereignly within the Church to restore a biblical truth back to its proper order and function. The overarching principle is that whatever has been revealed in times past, becomes our present possession. So, each restoration movement has restored back into the Church some of the truths that were lost during the great falling away of the Dark Ages, but it's been possible only through times of refreshment to break up fallow ground of the Church in preparation for the seed of the restoration of truth to be planted[17].

A cursory look at Church history validates this ongoing restoration. First of all, it is important to realize that many New Testament truths that were understood by the First Century Church were lost in subsequent generations, until the Holy Spirit began to enlighten these truths to his people, beginning at the time of the Protestant Reformation[18], in which the theological underpinnings were firmly established: the authority of scripture, justification by

---

[16] 1 Corinthians 2:13

[17] Bill Hamon, *The Days of the Saints* (Destiny Image Publishers, Inc., 2022), p. 65, 149

[18] Bill Johnson, *Open Heavens* (Destiny Image, Publishers, 2021)

faith and the priesthood of all believers. The Wesleyan and Methodist movement then introduced the demand for personal and corporate holiness. The Pentecostal and the Charismatic movement later profiled the supernatural work of the Holy Spirit in a variety of power ministries. All other functions like intercession and that of the prophetic and of the importance of teamwork and of the five-fold ministry were subsequently restored in the Twentieth Century so that we can surely ascertain that the infrastructure of the Church, so to speak, may now be complete and much more prepared to advance the Kingdom with the speed and intensity that has not been possible in previous generations[19].

As His Ekklesia (aka "church") has been in the process of restoration for nearly 500 years in preparation for all these things to be fulfilled in the future, it follows that all that has been restored to the Body of Christ, thus far, has been to enable each generation to fill its destiny and to make the necessary preparation for activating any other relevant truth that needs to be restored on God's schedule. It is to this end, we must receive divine revelation (viz. Holy Spirit enlightenment) already present in the Bible that we did not see before to be established in these immediate truths. With this we are not talking about things that are added to the Bible, but of an

---

[19] C. Peter Wagner, *Churchquake!* (Ventura, CA: Regal, 1999) pp. 5, 110-111

enlightening to understand truths that were given by God, but lost or blurred in our understanding by subsequent generations.

Consequently, if each restoration movement builds upon the prior one, we will discover that the Church has always been central to God's eternal purpose, as much as the foundation of any building sets the parameters for what is to be built. Indeed, the safety and integrity of any building is founded on the principle that the building itself must stay true to the proper foundation. Everything built upon that foundation must live in honor of those same boundaries and values. The foundation is designed to take greater weight; therefore, it must be built upon to take the structure to higher levels; therefore, God always takes us from glory to glory[20]. The careful master builder, the God of the ages, the Ancient of Days, is in the work of restitution and of returning all things corrected, amended and repaired, pertaining to His eternal purpose.

Consider this, for example, the Pilgrim Fathers[21]. They did not claim to have arrived at a final understanding of all truth; they were on a pilgrimage, looking for the further revelation of truth that lay ahead as they walked in obedience to truth already received.

---

[20] Bill Johnson, ibid

[21] https://www.britannica.com/topic/Pilgrim-Fathers

They came as near the primitive, original pattern of the first churches as any other churches of these later times have done[22].

Today, a new spiritual rain is descending upon the Body of Christ in these last days allowing its growth to maturity, "*unto a perfect man, to the measure of the stature of the fulness of Christ*" (Eph. 4:13). In our endeavors we need to see Jesus delegating His power of attorney to His Ekklesia for the performance of His eternal purpose as He's continuing to give Himself to His Church time after time in restoration. He will continue until His Bride reaches her ultimate destination. Let us take heart and believe for restoration in order to perceive that the Lord never begins a thing if He does not propose to finish it. He will see the *two families* (Jeremiah 33:24) being reunited as a whole nation—this will be a marvel to behold.

The prophet Jeremiah said that "*In the latter days you will consider it*" (Jeremiah 30:24). This very coming together as one, "*that the Gentiles should be fellow heirs of the same body*" (Ephesians 3:6) has been the subject of consideration of the apostle Paul in the preaching of the mystery of Christ and His Ekklesia. As Dr. Garr articulates:

> "The focal point of the divine revelation through Apostolic and prophetic insight in Paul's day was the understanding that God would bring gentiles into full fellowship with the

---

[22] Derek Prince, *Shaping History Through Prayer & Fasting* (Whitaker House, 1973), p. 155, 158.

Jews in the same body, the community of the Messiah, as the one new humanity. In this respect, the Great Commission commanded the inclusion of the gentiles in the covenant community of Israel ("Go therefore and make disciples of all the nations, baptizing them in the name of the Father and of the Son and of the Holy Spirit" – Matthew 28:18)[23].

It is this community of the Messiah to which the author in the book of Hebrews refers to when he says of Moses in order to be faithful in "***all His house***" (Hebrews 3:2,5), such as it is Christ "*as a Son over* ***His house***" (Hebrews 3:6). The word *house* comes from the Greek *oikos*, meaning a dwelling (literal or figurative), by implication, a family[24]. Therefore, in harmony with God's eternal purpose, ***His house***, God's house, is precisely what is meant by "***The general assembly and church***[25] *of the firstborn*" (Hebrews 12:23), the "***congregation*** (Ekklesia) *in the wilderness*" (Acts 7:38). It is into this very family that God was pleased to place you.

---

[23] John Garr, *The Church Dynamic* (Golden Key Press 2019) p. 421

[24] (Strong's Concordance #G3624)

[25] "church" used here is the Greek word: "ekklesia" (or "ecclesia"). The primary origin of the word is derived from the "democratic assembly" in Greek polity dating back some 600 years before Christ. It is used most commonly to depict the contributory/participatory nature of the early assemblies of believers in Yeshua. Other uses of "ekklesia" are found in Acts 7:38 ("*congregation* in the wilderness" by Stephen); a "secular" ekklesia/assembly (Acts 19:32, 39-41)—one "lawful" and the other "unlawful" but both described as "ekklesia"; and finally, the "*ekklesia of the firstborn ones found in heaven*" recorded in Hebrews 12:22-23 comprised of all saints in the OT and NT, as well as the "angelic hosts."

In these last days, the Holy Spirit is bringing revelation into all that God meant for us to be *"fellow-heirs of the same body"* (Eph. 3:6). The expression *fellow-heirs* comes from a Greek word which means *participant in common*[26]. Can you begin to see it now? God is altogether eager to convey to you all the benefits, privileges, and the blessings of being a member in this great house that pre-existed before we all arrived and what is the extent of your full *participation in common* with all the saints, from both sides of the cross.

He is doing it through a restoration of the truth about His eternal purpose in this last hour. Like you, there are countless people who believe that the ultimate purpose of God is to restore the Church to one, to its original condition, as portrayed in both testaments[27], but this can be done only through *expressing* unity and

---

[26] (Strong's Concordance #G4789)

[27] It is the conviction of this writer that the *"great mystery"* spoken of by Paul In Ephesians 5:32 (NKJV): *"This is a great mystery, I speak of Christ and the church."* (lit. "ekklesia") is the climax of "divine mysteries" as follows: *"The mystery of God, Christ"* (Col. 2:2 NU – omits "and the Father"); *"The mystery of Christ"* (Eph. 3:4-7) wherein *"the Nations* (ethnos) *should be fellow heirs, of the same body, and partakers of His promise in Christ through the gospel"* – thus, the *"mystery of Christ"* is His Ekklesia comprised of both the Jew and the Gentile or both "Judah and Ephraim" – "Ephraim" as understood from Hosea 8 having been *"swallowed up of the Nations and is no more"*; and the *"great mystery"* which is Christ and the Ekklesia found in Ephesians 5:32 (combining the Mystery of God, Christ and the Mystery of Christ, His Ekklesia described as the *"Great Mystery: Christ and His Ekklesia"*). (See also: Col. 4:3: *"Mystery of Christ"*; Col. 1:26-27) *" . . .the mystery . . . hidden from ages and from generations, but now has been revealed to His saints . . . the riches of the glory of this mystery among the Nations: which is Christ in you"* – this is actually the *"Great Mystery"* in that it involves both *"Christ in you"* and the perfecting of *"every man"* (obviously both Jew and Greek/Gentile) *"in Christ Jesus"* – thus, *"Christ and His Ekklesia."*

fellowship between its components. We will examine this in the next chapter.

Chapter 2

God's Eternal Purpose

The letter to the Ephesians is the Apostle Paul's masterful presentation of God's eternal purpose unequivocally set forth in a way that it would become impossible for it not to be recognized. After having laid it out in clear terms, in Ephesians 3, he clearly submits that its whole subject is based upon one underlying axiom and represents " . . . ***the eternal purpose which He accomplished in Christ Jesus our Lord***" (Eph. 3:11).

This is the same epistle in which Paul lays out the theological roadmap for the understanding of the dynamics involved in spiritual warfare through the lens of a man who was engaged in contending for the truth previously revealed; to wit:

> "*Put on the whole armor of God, that you may be able to stand against the wiles of the devil*" (Ephesians 6:11).

We need to realize that this truth is the target of demonic opposition hurled by spiritual powers of wickedness which continually aim at hiding it; so that it seems these legions of demonic spirits swirling around the mysteries contained in the Bible are trying to impede the knowledge of this cardinal truth, surrounding it by a gulf of ignorance serving as a great divide. Wrapped in eerie darkness, they operate in murky shadows cobbling together all sorts of malignant and poisonous weeds full of lies in hopes of not getting caught. Everything is a dramatic ruse in attempting to win, even for a period, the ultimate clash between light and darkness. But what was the truth that was so disputed so much so that Paul had to make a specific prayer request in his favor in Ephesians 6 (more on this later)? "We are now going to uncover it."

When we look at the New-Greek-Testament word for ***purpose*** (*prothesis*[28]), it denotes a setting forth, proposal, or intention. It originates from a root verb which means *to place before, to exhibit*. It can also signify *to purpose, or to plan, therefore, a setting forth, an exposition, a placing in view, or, to openly display something.*

Paul, through the Holy Spirit, used this all-inclusive and meaningful word because it fitly represented the heavenly revelation he had received, which now he is displaying in his address to the Ephesians—not sparing the opportunity of leaving a legacy to any future generation, choosing to leave nothing behind. Like a pen of a skillful writer, his soul overflowed with a good theme (Psalm 45:1) and he did it in a most masterful way, inasmuch that here we are before the very "***Wisdom of God in a mystery***" (I Corinthians 2:6), so to speak, such that it can only be received by one through the enlightenment of the Holy Spirit.

---

[28] (Strong concordance #G4286)

In placing emphasis on God's purpose Paul remarks that it is ***eternal***; hence, before time was, perpetual and from eternity past. Wrought in the Father and fully ideated, finished, and ***accomplished*** in Christ Jesus. Yes, accomplished! What an evocative word. It comes from the Greek *poie*[29] which means *to execute, to make to cause, to exist, to bring about, to beget, to bring forth,* as spoken of *generating power.* But it is also used to denote *to bear.* Simply put, Jesus/Yeshua the Messiah, has become for us the bearer of the **eternal purpose** of which He is the designer in person. This everlasting plan, stemming directly from Christ Jesus, ". . . *with whom there is no variation or shadow of turning*" (James 1:17), will last as long as time shall be, and be visually manifested in the New Jerusalem, as the apex of God's manifold wisdom.

In context, Paul links God's purpose with a mystery that has been hidden from the beginning of the ages when he says:

> *"To me, who am less than the least of all the saints, this grace was given, that I should preach among the Gentiles the unsearchable riches of Christ, and make all see what is the* ***fellowship of the mystery, which from the beginning of the ages has been***

[29] (Strong's concordance #G4160)

> ***hidden in God*** *who created all things through Jesus Christ*" (Ephesians 3:8-9).

With this remarkable statement the apostle speaks of a measure of grace he had received by God the Creator to delve into a mystery (from the Greek *musterion*[30], denoting *a hidden purpose* or *counsel*) that had been hidden for ages, dating back to the creation of heaven and earth, which was there for Him to be deciphered and unraveled for all listening ears to grasp. To magnify the unsearchable riches found in Christ, Paul recognize that the dignity of this sacred office evoked his utter unworthiness; nevertheless, he was conscious to be the recipient of a revelation that would forever change the perspective about the dynamics involving the beneficiaries of the New Covenant, which the Lord had inaugurated through His death, but was now being revealed in Christ Jesus. This was at the core of his calling as an apostle of Jesus Christ, who, possessing a unique mantle of anointing was being endowed with a weighty mandate and sent out as a true *shaliach* (apostle in Hebrew) with a dispatch to carry.

This he did, faithfully turning over to all of us the revelatory knowledge of those blessings kept sealed from time immemorial, but now was being made available to His Ekklesia He said He would

---

[30] (Strong's concordance #G3466)

build in full display. I don't know how you feel about this, but to know that through Jesus Christ access is given to a then-unknown mystery (now made known through revelation), makes me beyond thrilled. Yet God has given to us this honor and He tells us that it's ours for the taking, right there, to be searched out in the Scriptures of truth, beginning from the revelation contained in these apostolic writing.

No wonder that some commentators consider it to be the grandest of all the Pauline letters, earning the title of *Epistle of the Ascension*[31] because it tarries largely among the heavenlies and lifts us into eternity past, and for no other reason than that the truths enshrined in it are to be considered foundational in the understanding of the marvel that God has established in His eternal purpose (Ephesians 3:11). Thus, where once there were a privileged and separated ethnic people (viz. the 12 Tribes of Israel), now it is fully revealed—this hidden mystery of ages past—concerning the complete fellowship between Jews and Gentiles in Messiah within the Commonwealth of Israel (Ephesians 2:12). Chrysostom, an important early church father speaks of Ephesians as being *full of sublime thoughts and doctrines. It abounds with sentiments of overwhelming loftiness and grandeur*, one in which Paul expounds,

---

[31] S.D.F. Salmond, *The Epistles to the Ephesians – The Expositor's Greek Testament* (Eerdmans Publishing Company, Grand Rapids, Michigan)

thoughts which he scarcely so much as utters anywhere else, he here plainly declares[32].

Dip into Hebraic and Christian theology and you will find it is rich in revelatory truth; however, the letter to the Ephesians is by far the New Testament message that stands at the forefront in enlightening and conveying to all, "*and to make all see what is the **fellowship** of the mystery, which from the beginning of the ages has been hidden in God who created all things through Jesus Christ*" (Eph. 3:9).

Now, before expanding on the meaning of the word *fellowship*, I'd like to dwell on another element which is central to the revelation of the truth that clarifies Paul's definition of what that mystery is all about, which he had previously unraveled in the epistle to the Ephesians. Thus we read that, "*. . . therefore remember that you, once gentiles in the flesh–who are called uncircumcision but what is called the circumcision made in the flesh by hands–that at that time you were without Christ, **being aliens from the Commonwealth of Israel** and strangers from the covenants of promise, having no hope and without God in the world. **But now in Christ Jesus you who once were far off have been brought near by the blood of Christ***" (Ephesians 2:11-13).

[32] Christopher Rowland and Christopher R.A. Morray Jones - *The Mystery of God: Early Jewish Mysticism and the New Testament* (Brill, 2009)

This is more than a statement. It is a declaration about the definition of God's eternal purpose in Christ Jesus for the uniting and reconciling of the most two-opposing and diametrically opposite groups of people (Jews and Gentiles) in New Testament times. This had been a mystery all along, says Paul, and from this point on, Paul's train of thought continues, leading to a fuller exposition of the mystery he was called to reveal. But it is when he says that his calling was "***to make all see what is the fellowship of the mystery***" that his message becomes fraught with deep meaning as to our participation or share in this mystery.

You see, it is one thing to possess head knowledge of something, but quite another thing to live out the benefit and the blessing that comes from that knowledge.

Paul already made it very clear that through the blood of Messiah we, the called out from among the nations (aka Gentiles), came to be citizens of the Commonwealth of Israel, inhabiting and residing in a spiritual kingdom/nation/Commonwealth (Grk. πολιτεία or *politeia* from Strong's 4177 from whence *citizenship* or *citizen* or *polity*) that goes by the name of Israel; having a lot and a share in the great *household of God* (Eph. 2:19) whereby we have an obligation, a constitutional one, to enjoy *koinonia*, to have fellowship, with its constituents or citizens (*politeia*).

The Complete Jewish Bible makes the concept even clearer, where it says:

> "*. . . You were estranged from* ***the national life of Israel*** *. . . But now . . .* " (Eph. 2:12-13 CJB).

For Paul, **fellowship** and **Commonwealth** abide within the same range of meaning, having the same implication, and are not mutually exclusive. It follows that all constituents of a community living in a *politeia* (again, the Greek word for Commonwealth) or *polity*, cannot consider to be equally sharing the same privileges to the detriment of *koinonia*/fellowship with one another as it's all about a common national life!

Inasmuch as a revelation *per sè* is not enough without living it, in the same way just knowing your collocation in the Kingdom of God does not automatically empower you unless you appropriate its authority and exert it. It's like having received a costly Ferrari as a gift and not being able to drive it nor touch it while it remains locked up in a garage. In our case, the key to open the door to living out the eternal purpose of God is through understanding our fellowship (*koinonia*) to the mystery as it is predicated upon citizenship that now (both Jews and Gentiles) gain full access to the blessings of the community.

> *"Now therefore, you are no longer strangers and foreigners,* ***but fellow citizens with the saints and members of the household of God*****"** (Ephesians 2:19).

In other words, in Christ, our entry is into full citizenship in the general community of believers, comprised of Old Testament saints as well as New Testament believers from both sides of the cross. Wayne Grudem offers an even more succinct conclusion saying, "The Church is the community of all true believers for all time."[33]

Allow me now to pick up from the concept of *fellowship* and turn to the original Greek to disclose a marvelous truth. It turns out to be one of the most loved words of the New Testament, *koinonia* (translated as *fellowship*). This is mostly used to indicate Christian fellowship in the context of a spirit of generous sharing as contrasted with the spirit of selfishness. It's the sharing of friendship, so to speak, but as for the ancient languages, there's more to it than we superficially can realize.

The famous theologian William Barclay provides another component to the meaning of *koinonia* by saying that the word is also used to express association and partnership, thus used to convey

---

[33] Wayne Grudem, *Systematic Theology, An Introduction to Biblical Doctrine* (Grand Rapids, Zondervan Publishing 1995)

a spirit of generous sharing as contrasted with the spirit of selfish getting.

Then there is another nuance in which it is used, and that is to express the idea of community[34]. Simply put, there cannot be a Commonwealth without a community as much as there cannot be a household without a family. A blunt and sterile membership alone won't suffice. It takes fellowship and mutual understanding if we are to see a well-rounded restoration of the truth about God's eternal purpose. This necessarily requires the parallel renewal of the relationship between its components, the dwellers of the household in their mutual sharing in the fellowship in God's mystery. Yet many people are oblivious to God's original design for fellowship within the commonwealth of Israel as to confine it within the parameters of their own way of seeing it.

Unfortunately, and due to the fact that many were taught that the church/ekklesia is a separate entity from Israel, even their way of reading the Bible is marred with ***Stigmatic Theology***, an expression I've coined to indicate any interpretation of the Word of God which is done in conformity to traditions, prejudices, stereotypes and filters, which can only produce labels, brands, and stigmatizing or categorizing one another. In late Sixteenth Century

---

[34] William Barcley, *New Testament Words* (The Westminster Press 1974) page 173

a *stigmatic* was considered a person marked by blemish or deformity. Today, Stigmatic Theology can only offer a deformed view of the whole counsel of God by way of soundbites and petty doctrines as a glaring impediment to the Almighty's plan and purpose wrought by the blood of the cross in making the two (Jews and Gentiles) – "*one new man – so making peace*" (Ephesians 2:15).

Unfortunately, like a man with a blurred vision, part of the Church has lost its way, and it has become disoriented, disassociated from its home. It has to do with our spiritual eyesight, like when we have an optical problem and there's a need for the "*great optometrist*" to bring focus once again. Despite that, it is interesting to watch those who adhere to a belief system that denies the House of Judah any *koinonia* in the Commonwealth of Israel always wanting to try to convert the Jews instead of looking first at the general purpose of God in wanting to reconcile them both (Jews and Gentiles) into the same household of faith.

The beauty of God's eternal purpose is that once we get the proper focus, we discover that in the New Covenant through the blood of Messiah we not only come into membership in the Congregation (church/assembly) of Israel, but, as well, we come into the citizenship of the Commonwealth of Israel.[35] But things have not always been this way. We'll talk about this in the next chapter.

---

[35] Dr. Gavin Finley in http://endtimepilgrim.org/2house.htm

Chapter 3

Fellowship in Commonwealth of Israel Disputed

In our attempt to unfold God's eternal purpose, it now seems useful to dwell on the background that let Paul define for us the nature of the mystery surrounding our inclusion into the Commonwealth of Israel. Subsequently, it's useful to look at the surrounding scene in which Paul found himself when he wrote to the church in Ephesus.

Given the context, the apostle penned his epistle with a strategic warfare approach and mindset in view. In fact, it is the opinion of some commentators that during his time in the city of Ephesus Paul had to change his tactic in evangelism after a revolt that had occurred there that put his and his companions' lives in jeopardy (See Acts 19).

Now, he and his team had previously turned the city upside down with signs, miracles and wonders in open display which caused much excitement among the masses to the extent that this "divine outburst" must have sent a clear signal to the forces of darkness in heavenly realms. Therefore, Paul's doings visibly became a threat that had to be dealt with.

With that in mind it is also important to understand why this revolt took place. In point of fact, Ephesus was the center of worship of the goddess who was known among the Greeks as Artemis and among the Romans as Diana. By turning the people away from the goddess off of whom some were even making profit by selling shrines of the goddess Diana, Paul and his team really caught the attention of the spiritual principalities and powers ruling over the city from the second heaven, which had influenced the society at large for decades.

As consequence, the story tells us that people assembled and rushed the missionaries into the city's outdoor amphitheater chanting for hours: "*Great is Diana of the Ephesians*" (Acts 19:34)—to the point that had it not been for the town clerk bringing order to the uproar, the entire team would have been hunted down and killed.

The interesting thing is that instead of leaving the city and running for shelter elsewhere, the apostle Paul remained in Ephesus as the Holy Spirit desired that he have time to review his missionary strategy. It was Paul's view their fight for truth had not yet been won as there was much to do than he could realize; therefore, he sought to chose to dedicate himself to teaching the Word of God in Ephesus with a purpose in mind.

That constituted a major change in strategic thinking and planning because, as Dr. Michael Lake[36] points out very clearly, "He realized what a powerful hold the principality had upon this area and spent three years in Ephesus teaching the fledging assembly of believers daily. The apostle to the gentiles did not leave Ephesus until the summer of 57 AD. One of the reasons that the book of Ephesians has such theological depths is that it was built upon the three years of teaching that Paul had accomplished from 54 AD to 57 AD."

I find this conclusion strategically important to the Body of Christ, a spiritual tactic to be implemented in our reaching the lost with kingdom assignment. Fundamentally, the apostle believed that equipping the saints with the word of God was priority number one and foremost essential in accordance with the good fight of faith. Simply put, when it comes to these basics, as the late Dr. Michael Heiser put it: *Serious Bible study isn't for Sissies*[38].

That is to say, the reason why the epistle to the Ephesians is so rich with fundamentals is because Paul could experience first-hand the Christian spiritual warfare is not against flesh and blood, but as he wrote his follow-up epistle to the Ephesian Ekklesia:

---

[36] Dr. Michael Lake, *The Kingdom Priesthood* (Biblical Life Publishing 2020), page 188

[38]Michael S. Heiser, *The Bible Unfiltered* (Lexham Press, 2017)

> "*. . . against principalities, against powers, against the rules of darkness of this world, against spiritual wickedness in high places*" (Ephesians 6:12).

And this fight is primarily fought with the weapons of truth wielded at the right time and space.

> Here we discover that the teaching that comes from revelation is a mighty tool for training us in handling the fight, whereas our learning of it becomes a means for winning the battle.

That's why, when taken in context, the mystery to which the apostle Paul alludes, turns out to be one of God's preferred fields of warfare He desires for our engagement—as per the following statement, "*. . .* ***to the intent that now the manifold wisdom of God might be made known by the church to the principalities and powers in the heavenly places***" (Eph. 3:10).

Did we comprehend this? Perhaps we've never given a thought about it? The Amplified Bible clarifies it much more:

> "[The purpose is] *that through the church the many-sided wisdom of God in all its infinite variety and innumerable aspects might now be made known to the angelic rulers and authorities (principalities and powers) in the heavenly sphere*" (Ephesians 3:10).

Please follow me. God's manifold wisdom, when displayed becomes a mighty weapon of spiritual warfare. Right in front of principalities and powers in the heavenlies, God wants the Ekklesia to demonstrate a spiritual reality that there is nothing that can compete with His wisdom. And this Paul states unequivocally regarding the previously revealed proclamation of the mystery concerning Christ, that "***He Himself is our peace, who has made both ONE*** (Jews and Gentiles)" . . . to the extent that "***He might reconcile them both to God in ONE BODY through the cross***" (Eph. 2:14,16 – emphasis added). In other words, if Jesus "***. . . having abolished in His flesh the enmity***" had in mind the creation of His ONE BODY (comprised of Jews and Gentiles) "***. . . so as to create in Himself one new man from the two, thus making peace***" (Eph. 2:15), isn't this a matter worth fighting for? Unequivocally: yes!

In Paul's theology, the Gentiles, were no longer "*strangers and foreigners*" (Eph. 2:19) in that through faith in Jesus, they had become part of the "*household of God*" wherein they were joined with Jewish believers in the promise, being knit together "*. . . for a dwelling place of God in the Spirit*" (Eph. 2:22).

Still, the language Paul uses can easily be overlooked, as Gentiles "*were aliens from the **Commonwealth of Israel** and strangers from the covenants of promise*" (Eph. 2:12). As a matter of fact, Gentiles at one time were, but no longer are strangers to Israel or the covenants (plural) of promise. Paul is not speaking of Gentiles forming some new body apart from Israel, but rather a joining in the common-wealth of the covenant people of God. Most controversial of all, doing so apart from circumcision, by grace through faith

(Ephesians 2:8), as sons in the pattern of believing, but yet, uncircumcised as was Abraham when he believed God prior to his circumcision having been justified by faith alone (Rom. 4:10-12)[39].

Let's return to what Paul had said and pick up from where we left off in order to secure a higher vista. Again, the Amplified Version will assist us:

> "*. . . and to make plain* [to everyone] ***the plan of the mystery*** [***regarding the uniting of believing Jews and Gentiles into one body***] *which* [until now] *was kept hidden through the ages in* [the mind of] *God who created all things*" (Ephesians 3:9).

The reality of the matter is that despite the Apostle Paul declaring that Jesus' death allowed Jews and Gentiles to be reconciled into One Body, and that they were henceforth partakers of the same root (Romans 11), and that they now enjoy the same privileges in the Commonwealth of Israel—yet tragically, scores of believers are still blinded to this reality.

It's so plain and true, yet many Christians today prefer to adhere to their preferred doctrine, buying into all sorts of ideas regarding a separation of the two—be it total "theological replacement" of the Jew or utter separation from them wherein as Doug Krieger states: "God has a plan for the Church and God has a

---

[39] Justin Elwell, L'hitameck (Ebenezer Operation Exodus Educational Bulletin Issue n. 15)

plan for Israel—but never the twain shall meet."[40] But if Jesus died "*. . . **that He might reconcile them both to God in one body through the cross***" (Eph. 2:16), why is it this truth is so seldom proclaimed? One thing is recognizing distinctions, another is never wanting to proclaim their meeting point in the Commonwealth of Israel (Ephesians 2:12).

And why are Christians still oblivious to the ramifications of this wonderful work of reconciliation? Because its implications affect, in the end, the broken branches (the Jewish people at large) . . .

> ". . . ***for God is able to graft them in again.*** *For if you were cut out of the olive tree which is wild by nature, and were grafted contrary to nature into a cultivated olive tree,* ***how much more will these, who are natural branches, be grafted into their own olive tree?***" (Romans 11:23-24).

You see, in his epistle "*To all in Rome who are loved by God and called to be his holy people*" (Rom. 1:7 - NIV), Paul has chosen the metaphor of the olive tree in expressing the oneness of His *holy people*. In his letter "*To God's holy people in Ephesus*" (Eph. 1:1) he talks about a common-wealth, precisely known as the Commonwealth of Israel; nonetheless, one's collocation in God's greater family household is in full view.

---

[40] See Doug Krieger's text: *Commonwealth Theology*, Chapters 1-2 in reference to Replacement/Reform theologies and Dispensationalism, 2018, Tribnet Publications

Moreover, while many accept Paul's assessment on a common citizenship between the saved among the Jews and those saved from the nations, not so many have still grasped the completion of God's eternal purpose in accepting that those Jews who are still in unbelief, are too, prophetically speaking, to be considered part of the greater "***household of God***" (Eph. 2:19) so as to forget that if they will persist till the end, they will be grafted in again at the time of the unveiling of Yeshua—"*The deliverer will come out of Zion, and He will turn away ungodliness from Jacob*" (Rom. 11:26).

Putting it in simple terms, ". . . by using the olive tree analogy, Paul explained how the goyim (strangers) could be included in covenants without excluding the native participants."[41] Hence, a great incorporation awaits the Jewish people, and we (those from the "nations") need to see it in the context of them being "mutually delivered" as we are in the end (Rom. 11:25-26) by the Deliverer who shall "roar out of Zion."

That's why we simply cannot advocate for separation, but for inclusion—Distinction YES (Jews and Gentiles) but Separation NO (we are One Body, one Commonwealth of Israel).[42]

---

[41] Jamie L. Perez, M. Ed., *Romans from the mind of Paul*, p. 248 (Writers Club Press, 2001)

[42] Douglas W. Krieger, *Commonwealth Theology*, Tribnet Publications, 2018, pp. 41-42; and Douglas W. Krieger, *Commonwealth Theology Essentials*, Commonwealth of Israel Foundation, 2020, pp. 25-35

In his article "*Israel and the Church*" Pastor Carlos Rios of Guatemala has written:

> "When we talk about Israel and the Church, they are two concepts, ideas, or groups that have been divided for religious and historical reasons and mainly because a biblical interpretation was interwoven that separates both peoples to justify a position on the second coming of Christ."[43]

This is why, to give an example, all the efforts in supporting the house of Judah (the Jews) in rediscovery of their promised land[44] and ancestry is to be considered and appreciated. All this in light of God's eternal purpose, which, in the end, never consents to disunity. Yes, there is still distinction between Israel (See appendix – Defining the Terms) and the saved among the nations, but never separation in God's eternal purpose!

This is precisely why its truth is obscured to the eyes of many by those entities with whom we wrestle. Accordingly, we fight for the truth when we openly talk about it, but those of you who are trained in spiritual warfare would agree that living the practical reality of God's eternal purpose, that is, bearing a living testimony before all to see, as displayed as the wisdom of God through His Ekklesia to principalities and powers, is indeed the wisest way of contending for the truth.

---

[43] Pastor Carlos Rios, *Israel and the Church* in L'hitameck issue n. 12 (Ebenezer Operation Exodus education bulletin 2022)

[44] https://www.jewishagency.org and https://ebenezer-oe.org

I'm not talking about validating some theory but bearing a powerful testimony of the validity of God's eternal plan. For example, through the practice of unity between Jews and Christians[45]. It is important to realize that in biblical times Jews and Gentiles were the most divided people groups. As Bible teacher Henry Hon writes:

> "It was a God-created division. God literally gave laws to keep these two peoples separated. This division and enmity could not be reconciled until the cross of Jesus Christ. He terminated the enmity (hatred) created by the ordinances given by God in keeping these two peoples partitioned in order that He could create in Himself One New Man, the

[45] Please note: I have purposefully used the term "Christians" juxtaposed to "Jews" in that by 200 AD the Jews who had not acknowledged Jesus Christ as the Messiah, Who was prophesied in the Hebrew Scriptures (aka O.T.), viewed "Christians" as Gentiles or "from the nations." Jews ceased reading the Greek Septuagint, replacing it with Hebrew to separate themselves from "followers of the Way." The term "Jewish Christians"—even to this day—would be to most Jews akin to saying "Muslim Christians" – in other words, it's virtually oxymoronic; consequently, the growing number of believers/followers in/of Yeshua/Jesus who are ethnic Jews identify themselves as either "Messianic Jews" or "Completed Jews" in that the word "Christian" still holds a contemptible connotation to many, if not most, ethnic Jews because the name is embedded in "Christianity" which for centuries persecuted those of Jewish extraction, and through figures like Emperor Constantine—who adopted Christianity as the "State Religion"—were determined to separate Jew from Christian and make Jews second class citizens of the Empire. Therefore, when I use "Christians and Jews" or "Jews and Christians" I am using this collective noun in this sense: Jews and Gentiles or Jews and Christians. Doctrinally, "Christians" are NOT strictly Gentiles/Nations but are seen by most Jews as Gentile-Christians. "In Christ" there is "neither Jew or Gentile" (Gal. 3:28; Eph. 2:11-22).

Body of Christ. It is in the Lord's Ekklesia where there is now peace between these two estranged enemies."[46]

"*How beautiful are the feet of those who preach the gospel of peace, who bring good tidings of good things!*" (Romans 10:15).

Prayer, once again, can make the difference in bringing about the practical unity in His One Body—the Ekklesia He is building. We will see how, in the next chapter.

---

[46]Henry Hon, *ONE Ekklesia. The Vision and Practice of God's Eternal Purpose*, 2018, pp. 123-124

Chapter 4

Prayer is God's Channel to Revelation

It's mindboggling to know that the answer for peace and unity among the constituents of God's household has been all along in the Bible, and yet, far too many people have not yet gotten the message. Indeed, if they have, it seems that only few are given to contend for this fundamental truth. In fact, for nearly two-thousand years Christians and Jews have been missing God's plan of ultimate unity within the Commonwealth of Israel.

The present conundrum which now faces the Body of Christ, despite the divine fact that the enmity separating Jew from Gentile has already been abolished; notwithstanding, centuries of this great divide between the two has created a false perception that this implacable separation persists!

It really seems that the enemy has been well able to dish out counterfeit and false assumptions of pure dichotomy between Jews and Christians (see footnote on pp. 33-34) based on wrong theology. Even a donkey can come up with a cobbled-up doctrine claiming that it is sourced in God. The false light has upped its game and it's NOT been gunning, in the main, for the lazy and the compromised. It is targeting those set-apart to stir up fights and divisions among the ranks of Christianity regarding these counterfeit assumptions of disunity.

Considering this premise, and following Paul's train of thought, we need to interpret the apostle's plea for prayer in

Ephesians 6 to be the fuel for an effectual ministry in Rome: "*. . . and* [pray] *for me,* ***that utterance may be given to me, that I may open my mouth boldly to make known the mystery of the gospel, for which I am an ambassador in chains; that I may speak boldly, as I ought to speak.*** " (Eph. 6:19-20). I want you to know that speaking boldly of this mystery is positioned here in the context of putting on of the whole armor of God which includes the extra weapon of prayer in this most quoted Ephesians 6 passage because its outcome is the revelation of the mystery through the empowerment of the Holy Spirit.

Let me shift the focus for a moment to connect and highlight the missing link regarding our understanding of the importance and efficacy of prayer in connection with speaking boldly of the mystery of the gospel.

According to tradition, the Apostle Paul wrote his letter to God's holy people in Ephesus while he was in his first imprisonment in Rome (cir. AD 62-64). His ambition had long been to preach in Rome, but little did he know how this desire would be fulfilled. However, God had prepared him in advance to bear the afflictions connected with his ministry (See Acts 9:16). That was why he told the Ephesian elders that he was going up to Jerusalem under compulsion of the Spirit, while "*. . . not knowing the things that should befall him there,*" except that he was certain of "*bonds and imprisonment.*" (Acts 20:22-23).

The Eighth Century distinguished Bible expositor, Alexander Maclaren, has offered a remarkable commentary to the book of Acts when he commentated that Paul:

> ". . . did not know that these were God's ways of bringing him to Rome. Jewish fury, Roman statecraft and law-abidingness, two years of a prison, a stormy voyage, a shipwreck, led him to his long-wished-for goal. God uses even man's malice and opposition to the Gospel to advance the progress of the Gospel. Men, like coral insects, build their little bit, all unaware of the whole of which it is a part, but the reef rises above the waves and ocean breaks against it in vain. In fact, we read that in the end, '*Paul dwelt two whole years in his own rented house, and received all who came to him, preaching the kingdom of God and teaching the things which concern the Lord Jesus Christ with all confidence,* ***no one forbidding him***.' (Acts 28:30-31). The '*no one forbidding him*' marks a great step forward. Paul's unhindered freedom of speech in Rome itself marks 'the victory of the word, the apex of the Gospel.'"[47]

Think about that.

Henry Hon paints the picture of the reality of the Church in Rome, describing the dynamics involved, saying:

---

47 Alexander Maclaren *Expositions of Holy Scriptures*: ttps://biblehub.com/commentaries/maclaren/acts/28.htm

> ". . . believers in Rome would have had even more of a propensity for division because of the diversity in practices and doctrines resulting from their various cultural backgrounds, social status, and preference of ministers who brought them to faith in Christ. As expected from the deep-seated divisions between Jewish and Gentile believers, Paul's main challenge was bringing these two groups of believers together in Rome. That was his focus since all the other divisions were simple compared to this. The building up of the Lord's one body depended upon the wall of separation being broken down. So, the challenge for Paul was to build up the saints in Rome into one body therefore Paul wanted to show them every believer has a common inheritance."[48]

This is a most important concept, but often neglected, that while in Rome, one of Paul's goals was to focus on bringing together these most divided people: Jews and Christians (see footnote on pp. 33-34). He was practically speaking, preaching the gospel of peace wrought by the same cross which gave us the gospel of the grace of God for our redemption.

This is in essence the practice of God's eternal purpose, which was at stake in Rome. Paul found himself under house arrest for the sake of the gospel; asking the saints in Ephesus to pray for him with all kinds of prayers and supplications so that he could speak boldly to make known the mystery of the gospel. You see, God brought Paul to Rome to address this unambiguous aspect of the

---

[48] Henry Hon, *ibid*, p. 119

mystery, as things were not so good in town. The believers in Rome were the perfect example of an artificial separation wrought by preferences and traditions of men. But in the plan of God things were not supposed to go this way.

The example of Paul's apostolic trip to Rome, in obedience to his call to be an ambassador bringing revelation about a hidden mystery in times past, shows us that when it comes to a revelation of something hidden, enlightenment from the Holy Spirit is needed. That's why he urged the saints in Ephesus with words like, "*And [pray] also for me, that in the opening of my mouth, **divine utterance** may be given to me to make known with boldness the mystery of the gospel*" (Ephesians 6:19 - Berean Literal Bible).

It is interesting to note that Paul puts forward this most important subject of prayer in his letter to the Ephesians only after exposing and explaining the basic tenets of the gospel as he does in his train of thought in Ephesians 1 through 3. In other words, he links prayer and truth together because not only prayer is dependent from the Word of God but as E. M. Bounds once said:

> "Prayer has all to do with the success of the preaching of the Word . . . Prayer opens the way for the Word of God to run without let or hindrance and creates the atmosphere which is favorable to the Word accomplishing its purpose. Prayer 'puts wheels under God's Word'. In other words, 'The Word

> of God is made effectual and operative by the process and practice of prayer.'"[49]

Please note that Paul's main request was for *divine utterance* to be given him from on high. When divine help is sought, nothing but prayer can come to the rescue. Not books nor blogs can substitute prayer. Prayer is God's way for opening hearts, changing situations, righting the wrongs, correcting errors, and building up His Ekklesia. This is coupled with boldness, intended as freedom, confidence of speech or speaking with frankness.[50]

By experience we know that a fight in prayer nearly always follows an illumination. Author Rick Renner justly said:

> "When you have received revelation concerning some area in the word of God, the enemy comes to attack almost immediately, trying to steal the word you have just

> Especially, the visual expression of the practice of the eternal purpose, which was to be seen in the realized fellowship between Jews and Christians in Rome, was predicated on the church in Ephesus being dedicated to regular prayer for Paul, that there may be given to him 'utterance,' or 'speech' in the opening of his mouth.

---

[49] E. M. Bounds, *The Complete Works of E.M. Bounds on Prayer* (Baker Books, 2004), pp. 67, 71

[50] *Meyer's NT Commentary*: https://biblehub.com/commentaries/meyer/ephesians/6.htm

embraced, Satan wants to make you doubt that word, so you are unable to confidently stand on it by faith."[51]

Bold plainness of speech was the more needed, as the Gospel is a mystery undiscoverable by mere human reason, and can only be known by revelation; therefore, Paul looked for utterance to be given him. He did not depend on his natural or acquired power as he knew that the shortest road to any heart was by way of heaven.

It seems that Paul couldn't make it without the faithful intercession of those believers in Ephesus on his behalf. This is very true as per his most famous quote on prayer: "*In Everything by prayer!*" (Philippians 4:6). By this I would like to say that just abiding in the nest of theology without seeking for its implementation is no guarantee for the disclosure of a given truth, especially if it is a mystery. Paul was not looking to persuade people with a blog on theology, so to speak, neither did he engage with hours upon hours of public debate in defense of the truth (viz. the Greek cultural disposition for rhetoric or the "*words of wisdom of this world*"—1 Cor. 2:1-5). Instead, he knew that time was short; therefore, he relied on the one and only weapon he knew to be efficient, prayer.

As I said earlier, Paul's exposition of God's eternal purpose was unequivocally laid out in a way that it would become impossible for it not to be recognized. Impossible, I dare say, although not always adequately and equally interpreted. If that were not so, why

---

[51] Rick Renner, *Dressed to Kill* (Harrison House, 1991), p. 127

would so many still not be able to see it the way it is? Well, dividing God's people has been at the heart of Satan's strategy from the days of the United Kingdom of David and prior thereto with the selling of Joseph into slavery.

In these last days, God wouldn't be seeking to resurface this truth if everyone already understood it. As I have said earlier, for nearly 2,000 years Christians and Jews have been missing God's plan of ultimate unity within the Commonwealth of Israel (Ephesians 2:12). That's why it is time we get a fresh revelation of God's eternal purpose and with resolve wield its truth to influence those pure in heart, allowing them to seize it, fight for it, and be able to stand with Him on His side.

To this end, God is not looking for intellectuals. He is willing to leave out of the equation the literati of confusion, and opt for the nobodies of the world to put to shame the wise in their own eyes; in fact:

> "*God has chosen the weak things of the world to put to shame the things which are mighty, and the base things of the world and the things which are despised God has chosen, and the things which are not, to bring to nothing the things that are, that no flesh should glory in His presence*" (I Corinthians 1:27-28).

You see, God has been calling the weak, the feeble, even the unskilled from the beginning of time when He needed to restore truths on behalf of His glorious Church. Few of those whom God called were the *wise* according to the flesh. Even more, in these last days, God needs candidates to bring forward His work of restoration of the *eternal purpose*. They will not be found among those who seek only to enlarge their own kingdom to the detriment of truth, but among the ranks of those who are willing to pay the price for sharing the whole counsel of God.

These may be those that God sent ahead, like pioneers or pathfinders who know well that this calling doesn't always look glamorous and comfortable. In fact, most of the time pioneering is treacherous, dangerous and very costly. Persecution, injustice, betrayal, warfare and despair can be at every turn. But heaven's perspective of success is very different to the vein conclusions of men of vanity whose god is their belly.

Furthermore, common people are often God's first choice when it comes to revealing His mind through the Scriptures. You may be one of them, a Daniel of our times, with your whole life dedicated to knowing the mind of God, "wanting to know the truth." Then, you are counted among those who are *greatly beloved* by God (Daniel 7:19; 9:23; 10:11, 19). Keep believing that He is going to use you mightily because of your love for the truth. You will see and prove that God has chosen you to bring balance into the Kingdom to become His special instrument in the restoration of all things for the end of the age.

Chapter 5

There is More

In my book ***Called to a Holy Pilgrimage . . .The Gathering and Salvation of the House of Jacob***[52] I dealt extensively on the regathering in unbelief of the Jewish people to the land of Israel according to the prophetic scriptures which spoke and predicted a return to the ancient land of the scattered ones of Jacob's descendants. Because of the covenant with Abraham for a promised land God has been showing Himself faithful in bringing home millions of Jews from the four corners of the world.

The prophecy of Isaiah records this most amazing prophetic utterance where it says: "*Sing, barren woman who has never had a child! Burst into song, shout for joy . . . For the deserted wife will have more children than the woman who is living with her husband*" (Isaiah 54:1 CJB). Jerusalem, with her children in exile, is compared to a woman who never bore child (cf. Isaiah 49:21), but God tells her to enlarge her tent and prepare many places for many children, saying, "*Enlarge the place of your tent, and let them stretch out the curtains of your dwellings*" (Isaiah 54:2).

---

[52] Gian Luca Morotti, *Called to a Holy Pilgrimage – The Gathering and Salvation of the House of Jacob* (Commonwealth of Israel Foundation 2020)

So, homecoming! "'*I was angry for a moment and hid my face from you; but with everlasting grace I will have compassion on you,' says Adonai your Redeemer*" (Isaiah 54:8 CJB).

Tenderly, the Redeemer brings back His children to barren Jerusalem. Promises are fulfilled, and the days of Messiah commence![53]

In my text I also shed light into God's sovereign move in all phases of the gathering of the children of Jacob: their return to the land of Israel, followed by a return to their God by means of teshuvah[54] (return) and finally to Yeshua their Messiah. This process—in its entirety, will have been a critical matter of consideration in these last days (Jer. 30:24).

---

[53] Jeffrey Enoch Feinberg, PhD, *Walk Deuteronomy!* (Messianic Jewish Publisher 2003), p. 114

[54] Teshuvah, from the Hebrew תשובה, literally, "return," pronounced "tshuvah" or "teshuvah," is the forsaking of sin and turning to God. It is one of the principal tenets of Judaism. Judaism recognizes that everybody sins on occasion, but that people can stop or minimize those occasions in the future by repenting for past transgressions. Thus, the primary purpose of repentance in Judaism is ethical self-transformation.

Maimonides said, "Even if a man has sinned his whole life, and repents on the day of his death, all his sins are forgiven him" (Maimonides, Yad, Teshuvah 2:1). One should repent immediately. A parable is told in the Talmud (Shabbat 153a) that Rabbi Eliezer taught his disciples, "Repent one day before your death." The disciples politely questioned whether one can know the day of one's death, so Rabbi Eliezer answered, "All the more reason, therefore, to repent today, lest one die tomorrow." (quoted in Telushkin, 155)

Of these considerations, the prophet Daniel wrote that in the last days "*Many will go back and forth and search anxiously* [through the scroll], *and knowledge* [of the purpose of God as revealed by His prophets] *will* [greatly] *increase*" (Daniel 12:4 AMP).

The generation we are living in is the one referred to in the above passage from Daniel. To expound upon this, I wish to take the concept of "need to know" in time from the Intelligence Community, where in order to guard specific security operations you may be handed orders with classified information and told not to open them until you reach your destination (which will be for your eyes only).

This means I am not supposed to open them until I arrive at the right place at the right time. These classified materials are not meant for anyone else to see. Spiritually speaking, we are living in the generation with a prophetic need to know. We are at the right place and at the right time in history where access to our Hebraic heritage and to prophetic understanding is now available, like never before. The secret still lies in the anxious running to and from throughout the Book--locating the key to the riches hidden but now made known for such a time as this!

Most Christians who look at the nation of Israel as their prophetic compass are like Daniel of Chapter 9. They are wonderful people, dedicated to prayer and fasting, called to make a difference through intercession, beloved of God and approved by men, except for the fact that they have not yet found the missing link that would enlighten them to see the whole spectrum enabling them to be far more powerful instruments in the hands of the Lord. In other words, they do not see that there is more to it than they realize. Daniel, as well, was intent and busy in praying for His people according to the findings from the scrolls of Jeremiah which would point to the Babylonian captivity coming to an end.

> "*. . . in the first year of his reign I, Daniel, understood by the books the number of the years specified by the word of the Lord through Jeremiah the prophet, that He would accomplish seventy years in the desolations of Jerusalem. Then I set my face toward the LORD God to make request by prayer and supplications, with fasting, sackcloth, and ashes. And I prayed to the LORD my God, and made confession, and said, 'O LORD, great and awesome God, who keeps His covenant and mercy with those who love Him, and with those who keep His commandments, we have sinned and committed iniquity, we have done wickedly and rebelled, even by departing from Your precepts and Your judgments . . . .. We have not obeyed the voice of the LORD our God, to walk in His laws, which He set before us by His servants the prophets. Yes, all Israel has transgressed Your law, and has departed so as not to obey Your voice; therefore the curse and the oath written in the Law of Moses the servant of God*

have been poured out on us, because we have sinned against Him. And He has confirmed His words, which He spoke against us and against our judges who judged us, by bringing upon us a great disaster; for under the whole heaven such has never been done as what has been done to Jerusalem. As it is written in the Law of Moses, all this disaster has come upon us; yet we have not made our prayer before the LORD our God, that we might turn from our iniquities and understand Your truth . . .. Now therefore, our God, hear the prayer of Your servant, and his supplications, and for the LORD's sake cause Your face to shine on Your sanctuary, which is desolate. O my God, incline Your ear and hear; open Your eyes and see our desolations, and the city which is called by Your name; for we do not present our supplications before You because of our righteous deeds, but because of Your great mercies. O LORD, hear! O LORD, forgive! O LORD, listen and act! Do not delay for Your own sake, my God, for Your city and Your people are called by Your name'" (Daniel 9:2-19).

We need to realize that Daniel was so focused on them returning to the Land; this so much pleased the Lord as he was greatly beloved for his passionate desire to help his countrymen. But then, something of extraordinary proportions happened, whose consequences had important implications for the understanding of future events.

Seemingly out of nowhere, the angel Gabriel himself showed up bringing to him a revelation of titanic proportion compared to the one he had just received. In fact, because of his prayers and dedication to the welfare of his people, Daniel was given an expanded mind into the future while still absorbed and focused on the **70 years**' prophecy of Jeremiah: he received the greater revelation of the **70 weeks** (destined to his people and to Jerusalem). We read this in Daniel 9:24-27:

> "***Seventy weeks are determined for your people and for your holy city***, *to finish the transgression, to make an end of sins, to make reconciliation for iniquity, to bring in everlasting righteousness, to seal up vision and prophecy, and to anoint the Most Holy. Know therefore and understand, that from the going forth of the command to restore and build Jerusalem Until Messiah the Prince, there shall be seven weeks and sixty-two weeks; The street shall be built again, and the wall, even in troublesome times. And after the sixty-two weeks Messiah shall be cut off, but not for Himself; And the people of the prince who is to come shall destroy the city and the sanctuary. The end of it shall be with a flood, and till the end of the war desolations are determined. Then he shall confirm a covenant with many for one week; But in the middle of the week he shall bring an end to sacrifice and offering. And on the wing of abominations shall be*

one who makes desolate, even until the consummation, which is determined, is poured out on the desolate" (Daniel 9:24-27).

The incredible thing about Daniel is that he received all this secret intelligence briefing in one prayer session only! The message from Daniel 9 came home: there is always more than we can realize. It is as if God were saying to him: "Daniel, the seventy-years' period of captivity is but a launch pad to an even greater set of 'seventies' of which you have never thought of. You are looking at the here and now, but there is more in My master plan for your people. Their end is not yet, there is more in store for them, and I want to show you the plan for the ages which has your people as leading figures. Know that I have determined the beginning and the end of their story, and I want to use you to reveal it to all future generations because you have sought for the truth with all of your heart."

It is in this context of expansion of the divine knowledge—"*In the latter days you will consider it*" (Jeremiah 30:24)—that the full restoration of the salvation on behalf of the Tents of Jacob (the House of Judah) is reserved for the latter days. As it was for Daniel,

> There is always more to grasp and to see through the lens of the Scriptures than we can realize. God is opening a new vista allowing us to get a full picture of the restoration of God's own multinational company of believers, from both sides of the cross.

so the Lord looks around to seek for people whose hearts are stayed on Him to reveal His heart and purpose.

As my dear colleague, Dr. Gavin Finley, maintains:

> "The Restoration of Israel is far more than the promised future epic corporate salvation of the Jewish house we see in Zechariah 12:10. It also involves the coming in of a fullness of the Gentiles. There can be no full restoration of Israel until we enter the 70th Week of Daniel, and the called-out people of God from both estranged and feuding houses of Israel go into the trials and tribulations of the final 7 years of this age."[55]

What a marvelous eureka moment that will be!

---

[55] Gavin Finley in http://endtimepilgrim.org/2house.htm

Chapter 6

Can you see it?

From the time of its incorporation under the covenant at Sinai, the people of Israel became a set apart people, a holy nation: "*You shall be to me a kingdom of priests and a holy nation*" (Exodus 19:6). The same concept is reiterated in Psalm 106 which gives another perspective to what the Commonwealth of Israel is all about.

This Psalm tells the story of Moses leading the people to Canaan; it offers a clue to the understanding of the unity within God's family and household of faith. It says: "*Remember me, o LORD, with the favor You have toward* ***Your people****. Oh, visit me with Your salvation, That I may rejoice in the gladness of* ***Your nation****, that I may glory with* ***Your inheritance***" (Psalm 106:4-5). People, nation, and inheritance are words to refer to the same thing, to a company of chosen human vessels, set apart for God and to represent Him before the nations of the world.

Peter then encapsulated this principle in the New Testament. Speaking to those in the nations who believed in Jesus unto salvation; he says, "***YOU are*** *a chosen people, a royal priesthood,* ***a holy nation*** *. . . once you were not a people but now you are the people of God*" (I Peter 2:9-10). There couldn't be a better presentation of our incorporation into that pre-existing family of God and His household.

Dr. John Garr takes the concept back further into biblical history by saying:

> "The Gentiles believers have always shared citizenship in the holy nation, the Commonwealth of Israel, which is constituted and sustained by covenant from the Lord in heaven . . .. For the holy nation is constituted by a covenant from heaven that incorporates those who are translated out of the kingdoms of darkness into the Kingdom of God's dear son into a heavenly Commonwealth of citizens."

Dr. Garr further comments:

> "Peter's declaration to the gentiles to whom he was ministering emphasized inclusion, not supersessionism, in much the same manner in which Paul explained the mystery of Israel's continuation as the people to whom the covenants and promises still belonged and as God's family tree into which the gentiles were grafted. The apostles always argued for gentile inclusion, in the people of God and in the holy nation."[56]

---

[56] John Garr, *ibid,* p. 137-139

Now, what saddens me most is that despite scores of books published about the land of Israel and the Jews in general, and countless conferences and seminars allegedly tackling the topic (which I absolutely approve and deem to be a necessary thing to do to defend in an apologetical way God's supreme choice of the Jewish people) the plan of God for the restoration of the truth of His eternal purpose, languishes.

In actual fact, our status of co-participation and equality (in terms of collocation) with the house of Judah within the Commonwealth of Israel seems to be theologically resisted, diminished, and obfuscated. Some teachers do so for malice, others out of ignorance, and some are simply oblivious because it is not on their radar. Notwithstanding this, there are few who pause and reflect before an important New Testament principle.

> *"Therefore remember that you, once Gentiles in the flesh—who are called Uncircumcision by what is called the Circumcision made in the flesh by hands— that at that time you were without Christ, being aliens from the commonwealth of Israel and strangers from the covenants of promise, having no hope and without God in the world. But now in Christ Jesus you who once*

> *were far off have been brought near by the blood of Christ"* (Ephesians 2:11-13).

A word search for *Commonwealth* provides us with its significance for it connotes *polity*, *community*, or the *State* and is corporate in nature—*politeia*[57]—, the relationship that a citizen shares with the State. It brings together Jews and Gentiles in accordance with Romans 9:22-24, which has a profound meaning:

"***Even us*** *whom he* ***called*** *not of the Jews only, but also of the* ***Gentiles***"[58] (ethnos – multitude or nations). Therefore, what Paul tries to portray in Ephesians 2 concerns those who once were aliens (we Gentiles) who have now been welcomed into a different kingdom—a United Kingdom—into which they (we) are no longer slaves or second-class citizens, but can now bask in a position of equality, taking our place and enjoying our new citizenship proper within the Commonwealth.

As shared in chapter two, the Complete Jewish Bible makes the concept much clearer, where it addressed the Gentiles by birth, saying that, ". . . *You were estranged from* ***the national life of Israel***" (Eph. 2:12 CJB). In other words, to enter into the Commonwealth

[57] (Strong's Concordance G#4174)

[58] (Strong's Concordance G#1484)

of Israel is to be blessed with the same life and promises destined to those who were near because of their status as children of Abraham by lineage— "*. . . beloved for the fathers sake*" (Rom. 11:28).

The statement that the apostle Paul lays out in Ephesians 2 is altogether clear. Every person saved, born-again under the blood of Christ, people from every nation race or tribe, yes, even people drawn out of the *goyim* (Hebrew for *nations*), moved from their previous state as aliens and strangers and foreigners to full-blown legal citizenship in the national life of Israel. In short, from afar, from a position of jealousy, if you would (Isaiah 11:13), we have been brought near to a position of co-equality. At the time we come to be in Christ, we are simultaneously put into the national life of Israel. This understanding is what removes the jealousy of Ephraim vs. Judah, without diminishing our love and service for the House of Judah/Jacob.

Granted, rightly perceiving our POSITION in the Commonwealth of Israel aims at dismantling both Replacement Theology's summation of Jewry and Dispensationalism's implacable separation of the Jews, as both systems abrogate the relationship between Israel and the Ekklesia. In fact, "***He Himself is our peace, who has made both one, and has broken down the middle wall of separation***" (Ephesians 2:13). Ah, yes, but you claim that is only "IN CHRIST." True, but that heavenly reality is just as viable as being within the Commonwealth of Israel!

The work of the one who has become our Shalom (peace) is such that the wall that separated us has been broken down. In Hebrew, the middle wall of the boundary fence which separated us is *m'chitzah*, which literally means, "*that which divides something in half.*" Dr. David Stern rightly confirms what Paul said regarding the Gentiles:

> "They are no longer separated but can now join the Jewish people and be One with them as God's people through faith in the Jewish Messiah, Yeshua. Therefore, the partition is down, now the Gentiles can join. The Messiah '. . . *has broken down the m'chitzah which divided us by destroying in his own body the enmity occasioned by the Torah, with its commandments set forth in the form of ordinances*' (Ephesians 2:15—The Complete Jewish Bible). This enmity between Jews and Gentiles had four components. The Gentiles were envious of the special status accorded by God to Israel in the Torah. The Jews were proud at being chosen. The Gentiles were resentful at that pride. Finally, there was mutual dislike of each other's customs. In particular, Jewish customs were different from those of the Gentiles because of the Jewish people's response to the Torah, with its commands set forth in the form of ordinances, later developing into *dogma*. Simply put, the enmity or hatred sourced in this dogma has nothing to do with the Torah. In other words, Yeshua did not abolish the

Torah in its entirety, but the *takkanot* (rabbinic ordinances and dogma) relating to the spiritual separation of Jews and Gentiles, most definitely erected this hateful barrier, the '*wall of separation*.' Nevertheless, the middle wall of the spiritual temple is done away with forever."[59]

"*To create in Himself one new man, from the two*" (Ephesians 2:15).

"*That he might reconcile them both to God in one body*" (Ephesians 2:16).

"*Now, therefore, you are no longer strangers and foreigners, but fellow citizens with the saints and members of the household of God*" (Ephesians 2:19).

Can you imagine? We were once aliens; now, the sons of the stranger are brought near and included in the great community of faith, the whole congregation of Israel, with co-equality–distinct yet not separated—partaking of the covenant and blessings promised to Israel. This new spiritual status enables us to freely enjoy the special privileged position of those who have obtained a kingdom and a priesthood.

---

[59] David. H. Stern, *Jewish New Testament Commentary* (1992, Jewish New Testament Publications)

We who were once Gentiles have now been, through the Blood of Christ, brought into the Commonwealth of Israel, clearly meaning that such a Commonwealth of Israel pre-existed before we ever arrived. Spiritually speaking, now we partake with the Old Testament saints as much as we fellowship with any other believer in the here and now. It's a positional blessing, I dare say, where our citizenship grants us access to a broader fellowship because we have come to "*Mount Zion and to the city of the living God, the heavenly Jerusalem, to* ***the general assembly*** *and Ekklesia* [lit.] *of the first born who are registered in heaven*" (Heb. 12:22-23). What a positional blessing we have obtained through the Blood of Christ! Yet not everyone sees it or is up to it despite the remarkable words of Peter:

> "*But you are a chosen generation, a royal priesthood, a holy nation, His own special people, that you may proclaim the praises of Him who called you out of darkness into His marvelous light; who once were not a people but are now the people of God, who had not obtained mercy but now have obtained mercy*" (1 Peter 2:9-10).

Even the word *church*, as understood in the strictest New Testament sense of the word, refers to "*the called out from among the nations*" (aka the Gentiles or *ethnos* – Romans 9:24; Acts 15:14)—not simply a physical building or "house of worship." "*God at the first visited the Nations/Ethnos to take out of them a people for His name*"—

in addition to the "called" out ones from among the progeny of Abraham, the Jews of Judah, to be "*a people for His name*."

Literally, term used for *Church* does not appear in the Testaments; the normative word found in the original Greek New Testament is *Ekklesia*[60] (used for both *assembly* and for *Church*). The Ekklesia are the elect, the "called out" Jews and the "called out from among the nations"—together, they constitute the One Body, the One New Man, the Household of God.

---

[60] (Strong's Concordance G#1577)

Chapter 7

No Confusion Over Identity

What amazes me is that Isaiah confirms the reconciliation and restoration of God's own multinational company of believers, whereby light is shed upon another facet of truth where he says that at last ". . . *the envy of Ephraim shall depart, and the adversaries of Judah shall be cut off; Ephraim shall not envy Judah, and Judah shall not harass Ephraim*" (Isaiah 11:13).

This will be the climactic reunion between the two as they will comprise the one elect or chosen people. Before that happens, several considerations need to be taken into account. As said, we need to realize that the enmity between the Jews (Judah/Jacob) and Gentiles (Ephraim/Joseph) had four components.

1. The Gentiles were envious of the special status accorded by God to Israel in the Torah.
2. The Jews were proud at being chosen.
3. The Gentiles were resentful of that pride.
4. There were mutual dislikes of each other's customs.

All of this is coming to an end in the latter days (the time of the end) as God is restoring all things. I have personally observed this in my own experience, being a first-hand witness of it. Speaking of the envy of Ephraim about Judah, allow me to digress here and share from my own experience what I have learned.

Several years ago, my wife and I took part in a conference in a European country with international guests and people from different nations attending. The speakers were wonderfully gifted people of God; very humble, down to earth, and sound in teaching, but as it is the norm in large gatherings, we came across people we had never met. I remember when at coffee break a peculiar looking lady approached us who turned to my wife saying she had received something from the Lord to tell her. With an expression of excitement, she whispered, "The Lord revealed to me that you have Jewish origins," claiming she had a particular gift of discerning the Jewish identity of people in general. She did this in the hope of moving us to excitement, while on the contrary we were moved to less than enthusiastic—to her evident displeasure.

What I want to say is that these kinds of people normally start in sincerity, then move in naïveté and ingenuity for some time, but inevitably finish by becoming a fertile breeding ground for those who cunningly try to buy as many people as possible into the error of their sectarian and narrower position; especially, twisting and obscuring the true dynamics between our Hebraic heritage and Christian identity.

What I have found in my years of experience is that many sincere believers tend to look at the Jewishness side of things with envy springing from an inferiority complex, as so well-depicted by Isaiah in the verse I quoted. This envy toward one another (Jews and Christians) will only be solved (in their view) by embracing Judaism as a means whereby one can be fully accepted by God. Please do not misunderstand me. I wish to make clear my ministry is totally interwoven with the Jewish people and with the State of Israel. I work with and for the Jewish people. I try to love them as God requires me to do; I have a special affection in my heart for Jerusalem, in particular—from where the Lord called my wife and I to serve Him on behalf of the Jewish people.

Moreover, I am in love with the Land of Israel. I have made efforts to learn how to handle the Hebrew language, both in reading, writing, and speaking and among my best friends there are many with Jewish heritage. I visit Israel habitually and will continue to do it as long as I can. Furthermore, by God's grace, I will defend the right of the Jews to their Land and help them to make Aliyah, speaking on their behalf until death will graduate me from this earthly clod.

What I want to underscore here concerning the words of Isaiah which I have just mentioned, regarding the jealousy of Ephraim towards Judah, represent a reality which I have observed for many years—most definitely, there is a reason for this focus. It all comes from either overlooking or obfuscating our mutual participation (viz. between Judah and Ephraim), whereby Ephraim (the 10 Northern Tribes were "*swallowed up of the nations*" according to Hosea 8:8-9) was called out from the nations for the express purpose to be joined with the House of Judah, into the Commonwealth of Israel, the Household of Faith; thus, the manifestation of the entirety of the House of Jacob. However, what I have noticed over the years is this: hardly anyone dares to tackle this subject because it seems to be too complicated or difficult to understand in the eyes and hearts of many, but it should not be this way.

It is one of the simplest truths of the New Testament, yet one of the most neglected ones. In general, regarding our participation in the Commonwealth of Israel there is a lot of confusion and disorientation which comes from the false assumption regarding the status of the Church being an entity separated from Israel or subsuming the Jews, claiming that the Church is exclusively Israel.

No wonder this broken relationship has been kept in both theological and physical separation. This is a deep error and seriously misleading because it is based upon a medieval Church tradition going back to Augustine, Constantine, and, most certainly, Origen. Indeed, it can even to some extent be traced to the earliest of the so-called Early Church Fathers, let alone the adjudged heretic, Marcion (cir. 144 AD), whose principal goal was to get rid of all traces of

Judaism in Christianity. Marcion became known as the archenemy of the *Jew God*. Nevertheless, the Church as an entity found herself separated from Israel of the flesh—this is not founded upon any biblical truth whatsoever.

The erroneous theological concept that the Church is a mystery hidden in Christ in eternity past as an exclusively separate revelation given through Paul having absolutely nothing (aside from types and shadows) to do with the "***Ekklesia in the Wilderness***" (Acts 7:38) is a tragic misinterpretation, or, in sum: hermeneutical distortion.

> The "*elect from among the nations*" are brought into the Commonwealth of Israel —not separated therefrom. We came to be part of a Commonwealth already existing. Ours is an inclusion into an already existing community of faith and polity.

Virtually, my entire text affirms this theological reality. Similarly, the "*we the Church* vs. *those Jews*" attitude, is evidence of a broken relationship. The "us and them" approach is very definitely being taught from worldwide pulpits in the majority of evangelical circles (as well in Catholic, Orthodox, and most Protestant denominations). In fact, this has become so entrenched, especially in Western culture, as to create a neat separation of paths and destinies where the mainline Bible prophecy teachers proclaim that the Church has a separate role and a separate destiny from Israel and the Jewish house, including their nation and their Judaism—begrudgingly surmising that in the Eschaton (after the Millennial Reign of 1,000 years, yet future) we might find ourselves together as one People—that will take heaven to pull that one off—even then, the Jews will remain a separate people.

This system of interpretation has produced an unbridgeable chasm between Jews and Gentiles to the extent there is both distinction but irreparable separation. Moreover, those who adhere to this belief system are hostile to their members who show an interest in Hebrew roots—imaging and contriving all manner of heresies among those who wish to discover those peculiarities of the House of Judah/Jacob. Consequently, this persistent error in our theology has fueled the blood feud between the Church and Jewish Israel to this day.

All this feuding has blurred our vision of such divine duality between Israel and His Ekklesia (aka the Church). But as I have always believed, the Lord has called us to partner with God and be "*repairers of the breach*," (Isaiah 58:12)—the breach that comes from an ancient animosity going back to a rebellion in Israel that happened nearly three millennia ago; the breach between Rehoboam of Judah and Jeroboam of Israel which divided ***the whole community of Israel*** (I Kings 8:14 CJB) creating a split into two separated kingdoms (**Israel** - North, **Judah** - South). It is time to put right all historical wrongs and for Christians to bridge the gap that our forebears created.

In the following chapter you will see how this will be possible!

Chapter 8

A Kingdom Divided & Healing the Breach

Albeit great is the restoration of the children of Israel to their promised land and their subsequent national salvation (ref. chapter 6), the House of Judah—Jacob, the Jews—does not stand alone in the eyes of the Lord or in His plan. The point that I want to make is there is another and final restoration which runs parallel to the ongoing restoration of the Jews to their own land and to Yeshua, their Messiah—it is the restoration of the brotherhood in fellowship of the whole Kingdom of Israel, which is nothing but the reparation of the longstanding feud that occurred at the time when the Lord tore the kingdom out of the hand of Solomon (I Kings 11:31), at which time ***the whole community of Israel*** became a divided kingdom.

To understand its repercussions and ramifications, we need to go back to the reign of Solomon when Judah and Israel were one United Kingdom under him. God's original design had been for unity all along. In fact, at the outset of Solomon's reign it was clear to all that "*King Solomon was king over **ALL ISRAEL***" (I Kings 4:1). In those days, all Israel meant Israel and Judah, not cobbled, but embedded within, as it is, with no separation at all, rather, enjoying a full fellowship, and in total security—all 12 Tribes of Israel.

We read that "*Judah and Israel were as numerous as the sand by the sea in multitude, eating and drinking and rejoicing. And Judah and Israel dwelt safely*" (I Kings 4:20-21, 25). It was an entirely UNITED Kingdom, over which Solomon was established by God to rule and reign for David, his father's sake (I Kings 2:45-46).

Actually, the Kingdom was already united under the reign of King David which comprised all of the 12 Tribes of Israel, i.e., the 2 of Judah (Judah and Benjamin) and the 10 Tribes of the North (Israel—aka Jezreel, Ephraim, Samaria). It is central to the understanding of God's eternal purpose for unity between and among the constituents of His Kingdom. We are reminded that this community of people was known throughout the Scriptures as ***the congregation*** or **community of Israel**.

For example, when the temple was finished by Solomon, at its inauguration ceremony we read that, "*Then the king turned around and blessed* ***the whole congregation of Israel***" (I Kings 8:14 KJV); "***the whole community of Israel***" (I Kings 8:14 CJB). So, praying to God, King Solomon associated God's name with ***all Israel*** when he would pray to the "*LORD God of Israel*" (I Kings 8:20, 23, 25-26) as being the Lord of that ONE UNITED PEOPLE. Moreover, in King

Solomon's appeal to Him he would do it on behalf of "***Your people Israel***" (I Kings 8:30, 33, 36, 38, 41, 43).

But when Solomon multiplied horses, became an international arms trader, multiplied silver and gold, built pagan altars, he did so in contravention of what the Torah expressly commanded (see Deuteronomy 17; 11:7). Moreover, when he was old, his heart turned from the Lord, drifted away as he intermarried with foreign women and had multiple wives disregarding God's instructions (see Deuteronomy 7), so serving other gods.

He thus brought the United Kingdom into division with consequences that affected an entire people for generations to come. We find these details in I Kings 11. Pastor Mark Biltz points out:

> ". . . according to Solomon's wisdom, what better way to secure peace than by marrying the daughters of foreign kings? Even if it was his way of securing peace with neighboring countries, it was still a direct affront to God's command."[61]

Moreover, this was a direct violation of what Solomon expressly received by God: "*The LORD said to him: 'Now if you walk before Me as your father David walked, in integrity of heart and in*

---

[61] Mark Biltz, *Decoding the Antichrist and the End Times*, p. 113 (Charisma House, 2019)

uprightness, to do according to all that I have commanded you, and if you keep My statues and My judgments, then I will establish the throne of your kingdom over Israel forever, as I promised David your father, saying, 'You shall not fail to have a man on the throne of Israel'" (I Kings 9:3-5).

It came to pass that the Lord was not pleased with Solomon's breach of trust; therefore, He eventually tore the kingdom away from him to give the Northern Ten Tribes to his servant, Jeroboam. "*Therefore the LORD said to Salomon, 'Because you have done this, and have not kept My covenant and My statues, which I have commanded you, I will surely tear the kingdom away from you and give it to your servant'*" (I Kings 11:11). This was later confirmed by the prophet Ahijah, who was raised up to give a striking message directed to Jeroboam.

> "*Then Ahijah took hold of the new garment that was on him* [Jeroboam], *and tore it into twelve pieces. And he said to Jeroboam, "take for yourself ten pieces, for thus says the LORD, the God of Israel: '**Behold, I will tear the kingdom out of the hand of Solomon and will give ten tribes to you**'*" (I Kings 11:30-31).

In essence, a prediction was made that the kingdom would suffer a splitting, resulting in the Ten Northern Tribes be given over to Jeroboam, because of Solomon's forsaking the Lord.

But in His faithfulness, God pledged with Solomon that He would not tear away the whole kingdom from him, but would leave to his son Rehoboam one tribe, as per I Kings 11:13, "*However I will not tear away the whole kingdom;* ***I will give one tribe to your son*** [Rehoboam] *for the sake of My servant David and for the sake of Jerusalem which I have chosen*" and 1 Kings 11:35, "*And to his son* [Rehoboam] *I will give one tribe, that My Servant David may always have a lamp before Me in Jerusalem, the city which I have chosen for Myself, to put My name there.*" God had made it clear to Solomon that the covenant with David was for Judah (the one tribe), and for Jerusalem.

I'd like to take up the story from another angle to get to the same conclusion, since it is very important to have a clear picture from whichever way you look at it. The Bible tells us that after the death of King Solomon, his son Rehoboam reigned in his place (I Kings 11:43), contrary to the elders' wise advice, he exerted his authority to increase the treasuries of Judah by imposing upon the Northern Ten Tribes an additional ulterior weight, or yoke—additional taxes and labor exploitation.

Jeroboam, on the other hand, who by divine choice was to become king over the Ten Northern Tribes of Israel, fled from Israel when he heard that Solomon, his master, had conspired to kill him in that King Solomon did not want him to become king.

Then Jeroboam returned to Israel as soon as he heard that King Solomon had died. Subsequently, Jeroboam complained to King Rehoboam, in front of the assembled people about the expropriation of labor and the imposition of high taxes levied upon Israel by his late father; therefore, Jeroboam asked King Rehoboam to lighten the burden upon the people. Whereupon King Rehoboam responded to the Northern Tribes, after consultation with both the elders of Judah (who cautioned him NOT to levy such additional burdens upon Israel's Ten Northern Tribes) and then with his youthful contemporaries—who recommended much harsher treatment upon the Northern Tribes, telling them that not only would he not lighten their burden, but he would increase it.

The reaction of the people should not have come as a surprise to King Rehoboam. The consequence was that the kingdom became divided, and thus split into two houses administered via two kings. Sin, wickedness, and bad rulership always bring a divided kingdom, and so it was, wherefore the split was a rebellion by Israel against the House of David (the cities of Judah), because of the harshness of King Rehoboam.

Here's the narrative of the very parting of the kingdom in two. The Bible says:

> *"Now when **all Israel** saw that the king* [Rehoboam] *did not listen to them, the people answered the king, saying: '**What share***

BC to 537 BC) a portion of Judah returned to the Land of Israel—specifically Judea.

Meanwhile, the Ten Northern Tribes (Israel) were still occluded among the nations as per Hosea 8:8, "*Israel is swallowed up; now they are among the Nations*." The 10 Northern Tribes were not swallowed up by Judah, but were assimilated among the Nations of the Assyrian and then the Babylonian Empires.

In bringing this chapter to a close, I want to ask a question: "Where is the sovereignty of God in all of this?" If we look at this story with a natural eye, we would be quick to point fingers at this or that until we read that "*. . . for the turn of events was from the LORD*" (I Kings 12:15). Yes, the whole thing was from God to openly display His great **eternal purpose.** "*This thing is from me*" (I Kings 12:24), the Lord said. However, God never wanted an internal fight, since He is never for disunity, but He allowed the united kingdom to be split anyhow, because he intended to bridge the divide in His own way!

Think for a moment about the implications of this great divide. For instance, we know that God gave Jeroboam the Ten Tribes of the North (Israel), but the Bible sheds additional information on his lineage that makes us infer that there's more to it than we can realize. I Kings 11:26 says that Jeroboam "*was the son of Nebat, an Ephraimite*," indicating that Jeroboam was a descendant of Ephraim. Moreover, we read that Solomon "*made him the officer over all the labor force of the house of Joseph*" (I Kings 11:28).

Ephraim was Joseph's son, a grandson of Jacob. His name means "doubly fruitful" and is directly connected with the blessing of becoming a "*multitude of people*" (Genesis 48:4). This is to say that there's a divine thread connecting the scattering of the Ten Northern Tribes of Israel with their uniting again with their brethren under the canopy of God's eternal purpose. Yes, the Lord allowed the United Kingdom of Israel to be split because he intended to bridge the divide in His own way!

> To show His great purpose, God sent his son Jesus (Yeshua) to be the meeting point between Jews and Gentiles. It is in Yeshua that the healing of the breach takes place; through Him that " . . . *preached peace to those who were far off and to those who were near*" . . . (Ephesians 2:17).

The healing of the breach between the two separate houses of Jacob (Judah and Ephraim) was "healed" by the death, burial, resurrection, ascension, and enthronement of Yeshua. This is precisely the message of the restoration of God's eternal purpose, brought back to the original design for the whole community of Israel.

Chapter 9

Reunification of the Whole House of Israel

Now, the good news! According to Ezekiel 37, in the last days this family feud would come to an end as the Lord declared through Ezekiel, "*Son of man, these bones are **THE WHOLE HOUSE OF ISRAEL***" (Ezekiel 37:11).

> Please, carefully note, the "Whole House of Israel" in its context clearly speaks to the House of Israel and the House of Judah—a divine recognition of their distinction with the prophetic intent: NOT their separation.

Here we have a picture of oneness and inseparable completion. Then, with the use of a symbolic imagery the Lord prophesied that the two houses would be reunited as two sticks becoming one stick in the hand of the Lord. Precisely, the stick of Judah would be taken in the hand of the LORD with the Stick of Joseph, which is in the hand of Ephraim . . . "*and they will be ONE in My hand*" (Ezekiel 37:19).

> *"As for you, son of man, take a stick for yourself and write on it: '**For Judah** and for the children of Israel, his companions.' Then*

> *take another stick and write on it, '**For Joseph, the stick of Ephraim**, and for all the house of Israel, his companions.' Then join them one to another for yourself into one stick, and they will become one in your hand. "And when the children of your people speak to you, saying, 'Will you not show us what you mean by these?'— say to them, 'Thus says the LORD God: '**Surely I will take the stick of Joseph, which is in the hand of Ephraim, and the tribes of Israel, his companions; and I will join them with it, with the stick of Judah, and make them** ONE STICK, **and they will be** ONE **in My hand.**'"* (Ezekiel 37:16-19).

I wish to point out here there are many astute biblical scholars, researchers—both Christian and Jewish—who have either concluded that the so-called "Ten Lost Tribes" . . .

1. Remain forever lost among the Gentiles.
2. Were merged into Judah during all these captivities and became Jews themselves, while tangentially maintaining their tribal designations.
3. Are still being "hunted down"—researchers using modern technologies such as DNA and/or followed up by additional archaeological evidence.
4. Have been identified among various European nationalities and perhaps other locations among

> tribal entities in Southwest Asia, Africa, even Pacific Islanders or the Japanese.

However, and notwithstanding the myriad of conjectures as to Israel's Ten-Tribe whereabouts, there is a far more biblical resolution to the issue. The book of Genesis provides the background to this incredible prophecy which sees Ephraim as a separate stick in the hand of the Lord in connection with Joseph.

It is recorded in Scripture wherein Jacob adopts the sons of Joseph as he imparts the blessing over them. Before blessing Joseph's sons Jacob stands on the promise of God for his life: "*I will make you a multitude of people*" (Genesis 48:4). Rabbi Dr. Justin D. Elwell correctly says:

> "Ephraim and Manasseh are part of this family and dynasty of blessing that goes back from the living God on to their grandparents. They are the first children born in exile and the blessing goes to the child of remembrance. Ephraim and Manasseh were not eligible to be tribes counted among the sons of Israel because they were not direct sons of Jacob, but in the New Testament, we know that when the Lord calls he establishes no matter if we are born in the house or if you are

brought into the house, you have the same position in the end."[63]

So, Jacob says, "***Let my name be named in them***" (Genesis 48:16), "May they be worthy of having their names coupled with my own, and those of my ancestors Abraham and Isaac."[64] Jacob blesses Joseph's seed with a double portion to bring them into the Commonwealth of Israel. In adopting Joseph's two sons by Os'nat the Egyptian (Genesis 48:8), Jacob embraces the promise for a *K'hilah-a kahal amim* (the Hebrew for *assembly of peoples*).

Jacob/Israel insists that Ephraim will become a *kahal amim*. The blessing opens the door for the adoption of Gentile nations in the days following Messiah's death.[65] In essence and in inescapable biblical fact (not just a metaphor) we Gentiles/Goyim are from Ephraim with a Savior from Judah. It is what I call "the **blessing of inclusion** into the **Commonwealth of Israel**." It all began at the end of Jacob's life when he looked upon Joseph and his two children (Manasseh and Ephraim) and said to him, "*Behold I will make you*

---

[63] Rabbi Dr. Justin D. Elwell in *Torah 1 – Genesis* (Syllabus, pp. 66-67)

[64] Hertz, Rabbi Joseph; The Soncino Press, *Pentateuch & Haftorahs* (The Soncino Press, LTD. 123 Ditmas Avenue, Brooklyn, New York 11218; copyright 1960; p. 182)

[65] Jeffrey Enoch Feinberg, PhD; *Walk GENESIS!* pp. 212, 224 (Lederer Books, a division of Messianic Jewish Publishers, Clarksville, Maryland, 1998).

fruitful and multiply you, and I will make you a ***MULTITUDE OF PEOPLE***" (Genesis 48:4).

Dr. Feinberg sheds light into this instance in his commentary in that there is a great significance in adopting Joseph's two children by Os'nat, the Egyptian, because by doing so, Jacob embraces the promise for an assembly of people.[66] Hence, Ezekiel speaks about the stick of Joseph which is in the hand of Ephraim.

Now, with Jacob about to bless Joseph's inheritance there is a transfer of heritage in view with worldwide repercussions for the son receiving the blessing would, as well, receive the inheritance. So, Joseph brought the two (Manasseh and Ephraim) near to Jacob for the blessing. Then Jacob stretched out his right hand and laid it on Ephraim's head, who was the younger, and his left hand on Manasseh and gave the blessing saying, "*And let them grow into a* ***multitude*** *in the midst of the earth*" (Genesis 48:16).

Displeased about the reversal of his sons' birthright, Joseph attempted to manipulate his father's hands, but eventually the seed of Ephraim (from the Hebrew, *double fruit* or *fruitful* [67]) was destined to become that fruitful multitude of nations. "*I know my son, I know. He* [Manasseh] *also shall become a people, and he also shall be great; but*

---

[66] Feinberg, ibid

[67] (Strong's Concordance #H669)

truly his younger brother [Ephraim – fruitful] *shall be greater than he, and his descendants shall become a **multitude of nations***"—from the Hebrew - *melo hagoyim*[68]--(Genesis 48:19).

Eventually, Ephraim was destined to inherit the rights of the firstborn and is blessed with populousness (filled to capacity). This extended blessing would become the ***fullness*** [i.e., "***completeness***"] ***of the Gentiles*** (Romans 11:25). In reference to this expansion of Ephraim into a multitude of nations Hosea says "*Aliens would swallow it up. Israel is swallowed up now they are among the gentiles like a vessel in which is no pleasure. For they have gone up to Assyria like a wild donkey alone by itself **Ephraim** has hired lovers*" (Hosea 8:8-9).

To be swallowed up means to be wholly assimilated, so that now they are among the nations. It happened when God gave a certificate of divorce to the Northern Ten Tribes saying: "*You are NOT my people*" (Hosea 1:9); thenceforth, they were swallowed up of the nations. They never blended into Judah during the Babylonian captivity whereby they became Jews.

The so-called Ten Lost Tribes have been scattered among the nations after five Assyrian kings trampled them asunder during their invasions between 745 BC and 712 BC at the time of the final siege

---

[68] (Strong's Concordance #H4393; #H1471)

of Samaria by the hand of King Sennacherib. Author Doug Krieger has, on several occasions, written that over the course of nigh 33 years, the Assyrians deported, brought into captivity, somewhere between 10 to 15 million Israelites of the Ten Northern Tribes (based on historical demographers and in relation to the 1,100,000 "men of war" counted among the Ten Northern Tribes by King David, cir. 1000 BC—1 Chronicles 21:5). Yes, some of them returned with Judah when Judah was taken captive into Babylon, but only a small number returned[69].

When Jesus said, "*Other sheep I have which are not of this fold, them also I must bring*" (John 10:16), He had in view this amazing family reunion. Are we getting the picture here?

> God, in His sovereignty, has orchestrated during the end-time drama, by the closing of the present age, that the exiles, the captives among the nations (the House of Joseph/Ephraim) and the House of Judah (Jacob) will be reunited as ONE STICK in the hand of the Lord.

Here, it is important to echo at the time of the writings of the Hebrew prophets the Northern Tribes had not yet returned, still the Lord promises to gather them from the nations. In this connection I

[69] Doug Krieger, *Unsealing The End of Days, the Visions, Prophecy & Messianic Scenario of Zechariah* – p. 358 (Tribnet Publications, 2017)

would like to quote the late Dr. Michael Heiser from his groundbreaking work, ***The Unseen Realm***, because he throws further light into the latter part of Ezekiel 37 (normally left out) and brings the entire concept to the proper level of our understanding, thus, demonstrating the analogy of Scriptures from a well-balanced standpoint. He explains:

> "Part of the reason Jews expected a military deliverer in their Messiah is that the prophets had taught that the regathering of all tribes of Israel and Judah went hand in hand with the appearance of a great messianic shepherd-king."[70]

The passage at hand describing the restoration of all the twelve tribes by the hand of a mighty deliverer is the following:

> "*Thus says the LORD God: Behold,* ***I am about to take the stick of Joseph (that is in the hand of Ephraim) and the tribes of Israel associated with him. And I will join with it the stick of Judah, and make them one stick, that they may be one in my hand.*** *When the sticks on which you write are in your hand before their eyes, then say to them, Thus says the LORD God: Behold, I will take the people of Israel from the*

[70] Michael S. Heiser, *The Unseen Realm* – p. 364 (2015, Lexham Press)

nations among which they have gone, and will gather them from all around, and bring them to their own land.

"And I will make them one nation in the land, on the mountains of Israel. And one king shall be king over them all, ***and they shall be no longer two nations, and no longer divided into two kingdoms. My servant David shall be king over them, and they shall all have one shepherd.*** *They shall walk in my rules and be careful to obey my statutes. They shall dwell in the land that I gave to my servant Jacob, where your fathers lived. They and their children and their children's children shall dwell there forever, and David my servant shall be their prince forever.*

"I will make a covenant of peace with them. It shall be an everlasting covenant with them. And I will set them in their land and multiply them, and will set my sanctuary in their midst forevermore" (Ezekiel 37:19-26 KJV).

In this biblically balanced approach to the regathering, Dr. Heiser insists:

"In terms of biblical theology, this expectation was fulfilled in the inauguration of the kingdom of God and at Pentecost.

"Not only was the reclamation of the disinherited nations launched at that event, but it was accomplished by means of

> pilgrim Jews from all the nations in which they had been left in exile, now converted to faith in Jesus, the incarnate
>
> "Yahweh, and now inheritors of the Spirit and the promises of the new covenant. As Paul said in Galatians 3, anyone who followed Christ was a true offspring of Abraham, Jew or Gentile. Jews from every nation of exile had returned to the land to serve as catalysts for a greater regathering, the apostolic mission of the Great Commission."[71]

I find it fascinating, to say the least, because it opens the way to a better understanding of the imagery of the Exodus theme throughout the Bible, whose central meaning is that of deliverance and of salvation. The ***Dictionary of Biblical Imagery*** states:

> "The exodus motif was used by prophets and poetic writers to transfer the significance of the original Exodus to new situations requiring deliverance, obedience, identity or belief. As great as the deliverance of Israel in the Exodus was, Christ's salvation is greater (Hebrew 2:1-4), salvation of which the exodus is the forerunner."

---

[71] "*Who Are Gog and Magog, and What's So Evil About the North?*" Michael S. Heiser – ibid – page 364.

Israel and the Church (Ekklesia—Ephraim, and the "rest of mankind/Edom" if you would – based on Acts 15:16-17 and Amos 9:11-12) are in transition; however, the Exodus theme cements and bolsters the reunification of the **Household of God**. It is in the Exodus with its binary facets wherein Judah and Ephraim meet. There is a physical regathering and a spiritual regathering at play.

The Holy Scriptures only speak of just one elect. The full company of the redeemed are destined to be gathered as one united company. As we see in Ezekiel 37 they are to be gathered under the combined stick of Joseph and Judah. "*Out of Judah*" comes the son of David, who sits upon the throne of David. He is the prince of peace, the sovereign head over the kingdom of Messiah. He is the promised Shiloh to whom the sceptre of Genesis 49 belongs, the lion of the tribe of Judah. All of these unfolding wonders will be fulfilled in the prayer of Jesus in John 17, "*That they may be one, are we are one.*"[72]

> "*In those days, and in that time,*" *says Yahweh*, "*the children of Israel will come, they and the children of Judah together; they will go on their way weeping, and will seek Yahweh their God*" (Jeremiah 50:4 WEB).

[72] Gavin Finley in *Called to a Holy Pilgrimage* by Gian Luca Morotti (COI Foundation 2020), p. 277

Finally, the restoration of the Whole House of Israel completes the inclusion of the Melo-HaGoyim—the Fullness of the Gentiles be come in; thus, "*All Israel will be saved.*" Likewise it is altogether significant that in this restoration there must be a recognition that today's Commonwealth of Israel and the One Olive Tree have always included the "scepter" of Judah. This Commonwealth has always belonged to Israel; therefore, Judah (the Jewish nation) is wholly identified with their own Commonwealth just as much as they are identified "with their own olive tree" (Romans 11:24). Yes, the natural branches (Judah) were broken off in unbelief; however, ". . . *how much more will these, who are natural branches, be grafted into their own olive tree*" (Romans 11:24).

You ask: "How can the tribes of Judah-Israel participate in the Commonwealth of Israel when they aren't experiencing Yeshua's salvation?" Need I remind you that Joseph was rejected by his own brothers and arose from the pit to eventually be acclaimed by Pharaoh: "*So he* [Pharaoh] *set him* [Joseph] *over all the land of Egypt. Pharaoh also said to Joseph, 'I am Pharaoh, and without your consent no man may lift his hand or foot in all the land of Egypt'* (Gen. 41:43b-44). Thus the Gentiles of Egypt were all saved by him. "*So they* [the Egyptians] said, 'You [Joseph] *have saved our lives; let us find favor in the sight of my lord, and we will be Pharaoh's servants*'" (Gen. 47:25). Both his brothers and the "Egyptian delegation" sat at meal with Joseph officiating—they were separated the one from the other. Neither his brethren nor the Egyptians fully knew the identity of

Joseph—his brethren only knew Joseph in his relationship with the Egyptians and the Egyptians only knew him in their relationship with Joseph as their "savior"—these "unclean shepherds" were separated from them and unknown to them. Eventually, Joseph's revelation of himself to his brethren shocked them—but it was just as much a revelation to the Egyptians! *"The Deliverer will come out of Zion, and He will turn away ungodliness from Jacob; for this is My covenant with them, when I take away their sins"* (Rom. 11:26-27).

Chapter 10

Divorce and Remarriage

In chapter 8 I have given an exposition into the intricacies of Israel's "Breach of Jeroboam" when the Ten Northern Tribes broke off from Judah (along with Benjamin and the Levites—2 Chronicles 10; 1 Kings 11-12) thereby putting in ruins the Tabernacle of David known as the United Kingdom of David. Amos bespeaks of the judgment on Judah and the separate judgment on Israel (Amos 2:4-16); clearly, there are two houses.

So righteously angered was the Holy One of Israel with the adultery of the Northern Ten Tribes which ensued that He gave them a "***certificate of divorce***" (Jeremiah 3:8) but, although Judah was more treacherous than Israel-Ephraim (aka, Jezreel, Samaria), He did not divorce her (Jeremiah 3:6-12). Remarkably, Jeremiah, says of the Northern Ten Tribes and later of both Houses:

> *"'Return, backsliding Israel,' says the LORD; 'I will not cause My anger to fall on you. For I am merciful,' says the LORD; 'I will not remain angry forever. Only acknowledge your iniquity, that you have transgressed against the LORD your God, and have scattered your charms to alien deities under every green tree, and you have not obeyed My voice,' says the Lord. 'Return, O backsliding children,' says the LORD; for I am married to you. I will take you, one from a city and two from a family, and I will*

> *bring you to Zion. And I will give you shepherds according to My heart, who will feed you with knowledge and understanding. Then it shall come to pass, when you are multiplied and increased in the land in those days,' says the LORD, 'that they will say no more, 'The ark of the covenant of the LORD.' It shall not come to mind, nor shall they remember it, nor shall they visit it, nor shall it be made anymore. At that time Jerusalem shall be called THE THRONE OF THE LORD, and all the nations* (i.e., the "Gentiles") *shall be gathered to it, to the name of the LORD, to Jerusalem. No more shall they follow the dictates of their evil hearts. In those days the house of Judah shall walk with the house of Israel, and they shall come together out of the land of the north to the land that I have given as an inheritance to your father'"* (Jeremiah 3:12-18).

The Law of Moses clearly says that if a certificate of divorce is given while the husband is still alive, the woman, so divorced, cannot marry another—otherwise, she commits adultery. She can only remarry if her first husband dies (See: Deuteronomy 24:1-4)—otherwise, she commits adultery; however, if the first husband dies, she can remarry HIM! That is precisely what happened to the Northern Ten Tribes.

I am very grateful to Dr. Douglas Hamp who first brought to the surface this incredible and eye-opening truth, which I believe constitutes the key in understanding the dynamics going on here.

So, first, God gives them a certificate of divorce; then He says, "*I am married to you!*" How can that be?[73] Furthermore, this is all the more complicated when clearly the Ten Northern Tribes (aka Ephraim) was taken by the millions into Assyrian captivity over the course of some 33 years (745-712 BC) to the extent it is said of these ancient Israelites:

> "***Aliens would swallow it up. Israel is swallowed up; now they are among the Gentiles*** *like a vessel in which is no pleasure. For they have gone up to Assyria, like a wild donkey alone by itself; Ephraim has hired lovers. Yes, though they have hired among the nations,* **NOW I WILL GATHER THEM**; *and they shall sorrow a little, because of the burden* [lit. "oracle" or "proclamation"] *of the king of princes*" (Hosea. 8:7-10).

So, when did all this go down? When did YHWH (Jehovah) remarry her? When did He "*gather them*" from this place and that place throughout the world where they had been scattered, swallowed up of the Nations/Gentiles? And how could He ever remarry her who clearly played the harlot? Even if she married

---

[73] For extended research on this topic see Dr. Douglas Hamp's groundbreaking work on God's Divorce and Remarriage in *One in Messiah: Perspectives on Commonwealth Theology* (Commonwealth of Israel Foundation 2019) also @: https://www.youtube.com/watch?v=tyPYGgaDpek (Retrieved on 03.29.2023)

another while her first husband was alive, she could not remarry unless and until her first husband died!

Also, if her "second husband" died and she tried to go back to her first husband—she could not because then it would be considered an "abomination" (Deut. 24:1-4). In other words, for her NOT to commit adultery again or commit an abomination her first husband must die—only then can she remarry another husband.

Compounding her (Ephraim's) detestable situation, Hosea's accounting of her "state of affairs"—speaking clearly concerning Ephraim-Israel—the Almighty uses Hosea himself as His Own relationship with Ephraim and says to Hosea:

> "*When the LORD began to speak by Hosea, the LORD said to Hosea: 'Go, take yourself a wife of harlotry and the children of harlotry, for the land has committed great harlotry by departing from the LORD' . . . So he went and took Gomer the daughter of Diblaim, and she conceived and bore him a son, Then the LORD said to him: 'Call his name Jezreel, for in a little while I will avenge the bloodshed of Jezreel on the house of Jehu, and bring an end to the kingdom of the house of Israel . . . it shall come to pass in that day that I will break the bow of Israel in the Valley of Jezreel*" (Hosea 1:2-5).

But it gets much worse for this Israel—the so-called Ten Lost Tribes!

> *"And she conceived again and bore a daughter. Then God said to him: 'Call her name Lo-Ruhamah* [lit. "no mercy"], *for I will no longer have mercy on the house of Israel, but I will utterly take them away. Yet I will have mercy on the house of Judah, will save them by the LORD their God, and will not save them by bow, nor by sword or battle, by horses or horsemen.' Now when she had weaned Lo-Ruhamah, she conceived and bore a son. Then God said: 'Call his name Lo-Ammi'* [lit. "not My people"] *'for you are not My people, and I will not be your God"* (Hosea 1:6-9).

Just how bad can it get: divorced, no mercy, swallowed up of the Nations, scattered to the four corners of the earth, and no longer His people! Then a "cosmic change of heart"—so it appears—and we hear this:

> *"'Yet the number of the children of Israel shall be as the sand of the sea* [SAY WHAT?], *WHICH CANNOT BE MEASURED OR NUMBERED. And it shall come to pass in the place where it was said to them, 'You are not My people,' There it shall be said to them, 'You are the sons of the living God.' Then the children of Judah and the children of Israel shall be gathered together, and appoint for themselves one head; and they shall come up out of the land, for great will be the day of Jezreel! Say to your brethren,*

> *'My people,' And to your sisters, 'Mercy is shown'"* (Hosea 1:10-11 and 2:1).

The Almighty is either very "conflicted" or He has an amazing, awesome, glorious plan in healing this ancient Breach of Jeroboam in both remarrying Israel's Ten Northern Tribes and regathering them.

Indeed, he will multiply them abundantly, and then reunite them with the House of Judah and call the lot of them "**MY PEOPLE!**" So, when does all of this happen? Well, it has happened and is happening since Messiah, the Redeemer of Israel, came the first time.

First of all, as found in Romans 7, we have this remarkable analysis of "the problem" of marriage, divorce, and remarriage—in accordance with the very Law of Moses, no less, from Paul's own anointed hand:

> "*Or do you not know, brethren (for I* [Paul] *speak to those who know the law), that the law has dominion over a man as long as he lives?*
>
> *"For the woman who has a husband is bound by the law to her husband as long as he lives. But if the husband dies, she is released from the law of her husband.*

"So then if, while her husband lives, she marries another man, she will be called an adulteress [that's precisely what happened in Hosea's accounting of Ephraim-Israel]; *but* ***if her husband dies****, she is free from that law, so that she is no adulteress, though she has married another man."*

"Therefore, my brethren, ***you also have become dead to the law through the body of Christ, that you may be married to another—to Him who was raised from the dead, that we should bear fruit to God****"* (Romans 7:1-4).

Do you see it? Messiah, the Christ, even YHWH, said He was married to these Ten Adulterous Tribes—and gave them a "certificate of divorce." How could He ever remarry her? That is the great mystery! The only way she could marry again (the "law" or "covenant" of remarriage) would be for her first husband to die—HE DID. Now, we can be married to another, even to Him Who was raised from the dead. Her first husband died but was resurrected—she is now about to remarry and NOT commit adultery!

But it gets much better—regarding these Gentiles, Paul declares from Hosea:

> *". . . and that He might make known the riches of His glory on the vessels of mercy, which He had prepared beforehand for glory, even us whom He called, not of the Jews only, but also of the Gentiles?* [Note the question mark in the original Greek!] *'I will call them My people, who were not My people, and her beloved, who was not beloved. And it shall come to pass in the place where it was said to them, 'You are not My people,' There they shall be called sons of the living God.' Isaiah also cries out concerning Israel: 'Though the number of the children of Israel be as the sand of the sea, the remnant will be saved. For He will finish the work and cut it short in righteousness, because the LORD will make a short work upon the earth"* (Romans 9:23-28).

Now, do you see it? Ephraim-Israel has been restored to the "*Root that bore her!*" She remarried the One to Whom she was originally betrothed—talk about mercy—HOW GREAT IS HIS MERCY! And, more so, she is being reunited with the House of Judah. Yes, disbursed and swallowed up of the Nations—she now comes forth in "*twos and threes*" out from among the nations to be regathered with Judah. This is a heavenly reality even now for:

> *"But you have come to Mount Zion and to the city of the living God, the heavenly Jerusalem, to an innumerable company of angels, to the general assembly and ekklesia of the firstborn who are registered in heaven, to God the Judge of all, to the spirits of just men made perfect, to Jesus the Mediator of the New Covenant,*

and to the blood of sprinkling that speaks better things than that of Abel" (Hebrews 12:22-24).

Yes, the heavenly Zion is being united with the earthly Zion—to God be the glory!

Amazing Grace! The "Lost Ten Tribes" have been found! God's plan and purpose for both houses—the House of Israel and the House of Judah—will not be thwarted—they are UNITED as His prophetic witnesses!

Chapter 11

Rebuilding the Tabernacle of David

In previous chapters I have tried to prove that apprehending our position within the Commonwealth of Israel defines our identity as members of God's family. With this section, I'd like to bring the concept deeper than that, for I believe that our fellow-citizenship with the saints in God's household is not simply about a spiritual dimension *per sè*. God, in fact, does not save us just to give us a status, albeit positionally speaking we're enjoying the blessings of being seated with Christ in the heavenly places (Eph. 2:49). However, in God's economy, He also considers our involvement in the process of restoration to be part and parcel of His eternal purpose; especially, when it comes to rebuilding the old ruins and raising up the desolations of many generations (Isaiah 61:4).

All of previous comments read so far in this text were meant to bring our attention to God's intent in restoring His eternal purpose. There is a clear expression in the Bible as to what this restoration alludes. I am referring to the rebuilding of the Tabernacle of David. The expression, "Tabernacle of David," as found in Amos 9:11 speaks of a day wherein it says: "***On that day I will raise up the tabernacle of David***, [i.e., "the United Kingdom of

David"], ***which has fallen down, and repair its damages; I will raise up its ruins, and rebuild it as in the days of old*** (Amos 9:11).

Yet God will do so with human instrumentality, just as He always has done by stirring up the spirit (Haggai 1:14) of those called to rebuild the ruins of His Tabernacle once again. I believe this is the additional component to the whole plan of the Almighty. Then in Acts 15 the Apostle James uses the prophecy of Amos to be significant of the coming in of the Gentiles into the blessings of the United Kingdom of David.

> "'*After this I will return* ***and will rebuild the tabernacle of David,*** *which has fallen down; I will rebuild its ruins, and I will set it up;* ***So that the rest of mankind may seek the Lord, even all the Gentiles who are called by My name,'*** *Says the Lord who does all these things*" (Acts 15:16-17).

From Acts 15 we understand God promised through the prophet Amos He would build again "The Tabernacle of David," by taking out from among the Gentiles a people for His name. In other words, the rebuilding of the tabernacle of David [i.e., "the United Kingdom of David"] coincides with the entry of the Gentiles in God's family.

In Volume II of the Trilogy on ***Divine Habitation*** (*The Tabernacle of David*) Dr. Kevin J. Conner confirms:

> "James, the apostle, by a word of wisdom, quotes from the Amos passage and applies it to the coming in of Gentiles into the Messianic Kingdom and the movement of God among the Gentiles. The Church would be composed of Jews and Gentiles. It should be remembered that the New Testament Apostles are the infallible interpreters of the Old Testament Prophets. The Old Testament Prophets foretold the coming of the Gentiles into Messiah's Kingdom . . . God did visit the Gentiles in the house of Cornelius to take out of them a people for His name, as Peter had already testified."[74]

> "'***On that day I will raise up The tabernacle of David***, *which has fallen down, and repair its damages; I will raise up its ruins, and rebuild it as in the days of old;* ***That they may possess the remnant of Edom*** [LXX "Mankind" as per Obadiah 19 – even "Esau" or "Adam"], ***and all the Gentiles who are called by My name,***' *Says the LORD who does this thing*" (Amos 9:11-12).

---

[74] Kevin J. Conner, *The Tabernacle of David: The Presence of God as Experienced in the Tabernacle* (KJC 1976)

I cannot turn a blind eye to my Italian origin and say that I am very proud of my ancestry when I remember that it was to the House of Cornelius, the Italian band, to whom the gospel of the grace of God was initially opened—in point of fact it was this House of Cornelius which was the center of Peter's remarks at the Acts 15 "Jerusalem Council."

Also, in Acts 15 it speaks not only of the remnant of Ephraim (so implied in the unity of the United Kingdom seen in the Tabernacle of David), but likewise, "*so that the rest of mankind*" (Amos 9:12) may seek the LORD, even all the Nations (aka "Gentiles") who are "*called by My name*."

This allusion by James bespeaks of Amos 9:12: "'***That they may possess the remnant of Edom, And all the Gentiles who are called by My name***', *Says the LORD who does these things*" (Amos 9:12).

Commenting on this passage from Amos, ***The Pulpit Commentary*** sheds light into the meaning of *Edom* vs. "*The rest of mankind*" of Acts 15, to wit:

> "The Septuagint (LXX) gives us this: '*That the remnant of man may earnestly seek the LORD,*' regarding Edom as a representative of alienation from God and altering the text to make the sense more generally intelligible. '*Which are called*

by my Name' ("*Over whom My Name has been called*"–Septuagint)."

This is closer to the Hebrew, but the meaning is much the same,

viz. all those who are dedicated to God and belong to Him being by faith incorporated into the true Israel of God.

God has let us in so that we could have communion with Him as David did. He went in before us to demonstrate it was possible to gaze on the glory of God in the Sanctuary of the Tabernacle. Even greater would have been the glory that the Lord would have bestowed on us, the living Tabernacle of His presence. If you were David gazing on the glory inside the tent, what would you remember after you left? "The tent, the manifested glory of God?" It is the gazing on the glory that allows the King to be enthroned—observed as the One dispensing grace upon the United Kingdom of David.

When we look at Jesus, we cannot but see Him as the peacemaker between the two, *so making peace*. Jesus Himself becomes the very gate to the Family, the Household of God. So, not only do we come closer to one another, but to the most precious pearl of great value, the Root of the Olive Tree of Salvation, the entrance to the spiritual family, the mediator of the New Covenant.

An analogy of the building up of the Tabernacle of David can be drawn by the allegory depicted in Isaiah 54 where in her lowly estate, Zion is like that woman forsaken, widow and without child, yet is commanded to shout and sing, to act as a barren person would not.

> "'*Sing, O barren, You who have not borne! Break forth into singing, and cry aloud, You who have not labored with child! For more are the children of the desolate than the children of the married woman,' says the Lord.*" (Isaiah 54:1)

This is the whole company of Messiah in its embryonic stage where the prophet commands her to enlarge the place of her habitation. As Dr. Young remarks:

> "This is to prepare for the great increase. So, Isaiah uses the figure of a tent, for Zion is conceived as a woman who dwells in her own tent and is responsible to enlarge that tent."[75]

> ***"Enlarge the place of your tent, And let them stretch out the curtains of your dwellings; Do not spare; Lengthen your cords, And strengthen your stakes. For you shall expand to the right and to the left, And your descendants will inherit***

[75] Edward J. Young, *The Book of Isaiah, Volume 3* (Edermans 1972)

the nations, And make the desolate cities inhabited" (Isaiah 54:3).

This enlargement, this receiving of her sons, is nothing but the raising up of the Tabernacle of David, the incorporation of the Gentiles into the United Kingdom of David.

Chapter 12

Towards the Healing of the Envy

On the path to restoration there's a need to believe that what has been predicted will be, and that healing is part of the process. For instance, to give reason to what is prophesied in Isaiah 11:13 that speaks of a future time when "***the envy of Ephraim shall depart***," or that "***Ephraim shall not envy Judah***," we have to believe that this approach towards Judah, tainted with envy, will definitely come to an end.

It's part and parcel of the restoration of the truth concerning God's eternal purpose. Nevertheless, until that day people will still tend to see things from the outside looking in only, feeling out of the picture, perceiving a golden image of forbidden mystical aura around everything that comes from Judah, as if contemplating it from afar, not purposely, obviously, but forgetting an important reality that the moment they have been brought near, that in the moment they have believed God for their salvation; they have been given a co-citizenship in the Commonwealth of Israel through the ingrafting, and they have become fellow-citizens with all its members (from both sides of the cross)—holding a spiritual position of co-equality.

Sad to say, but the fruit of some people are evidently manifest in their walk with their fellow believers in the Ekklesia. I have witnessed scores of Christians who after rightly moving away from Replacement Theology (intended as 'the view that the church is the new or true Israel that has permanently replaced or superseded Israel as the people of God'[76]), found themselves totally immersed into another belief system, which I define as **opposition theology**, an expression that well describes ". . . the hostile behavior springing from a limited view of the Commonwealth of Israel that has caused separation between the group of the pro-Israel-only-people, on the one hand, and all others on the other, to the detriment of a balanced view and harmony between the members of the household of God."

To my view, this happens either because of a sense of inferiority and for the lack of a true self-identity. However, if people would just take time to profit from the Word for their benefit (remember Daniel 9 – There is more, chapter 5), they would discover with amazement that all the things given to the Jews/Judah were also extended through the New Covenant to those called out from the nations that believed in God. Then the Ekklesia would progressively

[76] Thomas D. Ice, *What is Replacement Theology* (https://digitalcommons.liberty.edu/cgi/viewcontent.cgi?article=1105&context=pretrib_arch)

find its lost path and the peace we so much desire, thereby keeping all within the same camp.

As Dr. Garr points out very well when he says that in seeking to reclaim our biblical Hebrew heritage:

> ". . . we must be careful that we do not establish a new elitism that brings judgment and condemnation upon those who do not understand these concepts. If we are to adopt a truly Judaic mindset, we will maintain tolerance for others, and we will shun the development of yet another creed that establishes another orthodoxy and further divides the body of Christ."[77]

The good news is that the envy and the jealousy are coming to an end. I am much more confident in the Word of God which declares that one day soon "*the envy of Ephraim shall depart.*" In fact, increasingly more people are perceiving a clarion call to go back to the complete Bible. It was A. W. Tozer who once said that "Nothing less than a whole Bible can make a whole Christian."[78]

---

[77] John D. Garr, *Our Lost Legacy*, chapter 19 (Golden Key Press, 2006)
[78] A. W. Tozer, *Of God and Men: Cultivating the Divine/Human Relationship* (Chicago, IL: Moody Press, 2015)

Thus, the Ekklesia Jesus is building to oppose the "*gates of Hades*" will at last awaken from her slumber to embrace her roots, partake of its nourishment, get back to the apostolic way—then signs would follow, revival will come, and many children will come back to its tents, while all carnal ministries will cease to exist.

Sadly, the scarcity of sound teaching in the Body of Messiah has caused many to leave her shores to embark upon a journey which has brought them to places where they still hunger for more. Another personal note. God called me while living in London (England) in the early '90s. I grew up in Italy (as a believer) primarily within a Pentecostal denomination where the motto was: "All the Gospel!" This conveyed the idea of holding all the truth. It did not take me long to find out that this claim was spurious, to say the least.

As years went by, it became evident that essential pieces of God's mosaic were missing to give credibility to the claim put at the forefront. This was one reason why I was inspired to pursue the missing components of the faith once delivered to the saints and to become a seeker of what I felt was to be a balanced truth. Thus, if I were to somehow recover the old paths, the ancient ways in which to dwell, a need for a paradigm shift in the way things were taught was needed and with a great dose of unlearning.

Today, we are called of God to work with Him in restoring the truth of His eternal purpose for the Ekklesia by presenting, on the starting block, a balanced view of the engrafting/inclusion into the family tree of salvation (Romans 11), which would open the way to further knowledge of our spiritual positioning in the great and general congregation of Israel via the new birth. In so doing, the envy of Ephraim can cease while the Lord sheds light into our participation as partners with the Jewish people in the covenant promises of the New Covenant—even in those whose vision extends but to Genesis 12:3 ("*I will bless those who bless you, and I will curse him who curses you*").

By teaching that supreme truth of our ***engrafting*** into the family tree of salvation, we champion **God's eternal purpose** and become restorers of "*streets to dwell in*" (Isaiah 58:12). To that end, looking back at **Abraham** is paramount in understanding our **inclusion** and in helping in the task of getting back our **lost status as citizens** in the **Commonwealth of Israel**.

The key to understanding the root and the branches metaphor in Romans 11 lies in looking at the Jews, the natural branches, because they boast a lineage derived from both paternities:

> Therefore, when Gentiles are saved by Israel's Messiah, God brings them into His eternal covenant. They get a change of status whereby they no longer are considered Gentiles but full-fledged citizens of ISRAEL.

they are the children of Abraham and the children of Abraham by faith (when they believe in Yeshua). Whereas, those believers called out from the nations, on the other hand, are called the wild branches because they are children of Abraham only by faith, not by birth. So, it is faith in the end that determines our inclusion, not ethnicity (Galatians 3:1-18).[79]

Jeremiah 30-31 paves the way before us the entire plan of God concerning this great restoration with the House of Judah being gathered to the Lord. His mercy has been shown to the House of Ephraim, the stick of Joseph (believers called out from the nations) whereby both Houses are included in the New Covenant—for they have always been so included (Jeremiah 31:31: "*Behold, the days are coming, says the LORD, when I will make a new covenant with the house of Israel and with the house of Judah.*").

It is through the new birth that all of us—Jews and Gentiles—take on our new identity in the Commonwealth of Israel (Ephesians 2:11-13). As Dr. Gavin Finley points out:

"Nowhere in the Holy Scriptures does God ever speak of two covenant peoples. Nowhere do we see one salvation plan for Israel and another for the Church. All who have been saved, or ever will

---

[79] Douglas R. Shearer, *Calvin on the Ropes*, 2009

be saved, are saved by the same plan of salvation. They are saved by grace through faith in Israel's promised Sacrificial Lamb."[80]

> "*Then at last the jealousy between Israel and Judah will end.* ***They will not be rivals anymore***" (Isaiah 11:13 NLT).

What a hope!

[80] Dr. Gavin Finley, MD, in http://endtimepilgrim.org/elect.htm. Dr. Gavin Finley is a pioneer of Commonwealth Theology and the editor of the website www.endtimepilgrim.org, a ministry dedicated to helping us in understanding the mystery of the Commonwealth of Israel.

Chapter 13
Get Them Out Of The Ghetto

I'm very confident in the Word of God; knowing for sure that if Ephraim shall not envy Judah anymore, similarly it will be the case that "*Judah shall not harass Ephraim*" (Isaiah 11:13). On the latter, "*Judah shall not harass Ephraim,*" we need to ask ourselves why some of those of the House of Judah have been hostile to us believers over the years.

Well, put it in simple terms, it's been because we have never done anything to approach them; we've never considered them; we have—in their eyes—stolen their promises and relegated them (i.e., the Jews) to a theological ghetto by keeping them spiritually alienated from us. If the Bible is for unity within the Commonwealth of Israel, my question is, are there any barriers today that prevent access to that mutual citizenship so clearly defined in the book of Ephesians?

On a similar inquiry Paul quotes from Deuteronomy 32:21 wherein the Almighty's anger towards Israel's persistent backsliding would one day "*provoke them to jealousy*" (Rom. 11:14 – KJV or "*Salvation has come to the Gentiles to make Israel envious*") – whereas in Deuteronomy we read: "*They* (Israel) *made me jealous by what is no god and angered me with their worthless idols. I will make them envious by those who are not a people; I will make them angry by a nation that has no understanding*" (Deut. 32:21).

In other words, this mutual envy between Judah (Jews) and Ephraim ("*swallowed up among the nations*"/Gentiles) appears to have been orchestrated by divine design! Consequently, God Almighty who designed it due to Israel's idolatry (found in Deuteronomy 32 in the "Song of Moses") did in point of prophetic fact provoke them (the Jews) to envy/jealousy by those who were adjudged "not a people . . . by a nation that has no understanding" –sure sounds like Ephraim of Hosea:

> "*Call her Lo-Ruhamah* (which means "no mercy"), *for I will no longer show love to Israel* [viz. Jezreel of Hos. 1:4 – aka "the Kingdom of Israel"] . . . *Call him Lo-Ammi* (which means "not my people"), *for you are not my people, and I am not your God*" (Hos. 1:6, 9).

As they say, this invidious business of envy and jealousy swings both ways. I mean, really, I can see why Ephraim-Israel is a little "pushed out of shape" over the Almighty giving Ephraim a "certificate of divorce" (Jer. 3:8) and at the same time "adding insult to would be injury" follows it up by this:

> "*Yet I will show love to Judah: and I will save them-not by bow, sword or battle, or by horses and horsemen, but I, the LORD their God, will save them*" (Hos. 1:7).

Really? Both Ephraim-Israel and Judah-Israel were immersed in idolatry. Listen to what the LORD said through Jeremiah:

> "'*In spite of all this, her unfaithful sister Judah did not return to me with all her heart, but only in pretense,' declares the LORD. The LORD said to me, 'Faithless Israel is more righteous than unfaithful Judah*'" (Jer. 3:10-11).

Just so you know, the LORD just gave Ephraim-Israel a writ of divorce and then followed it up by saying to Judah-Israel "*Faithless Israel is more righteous than unfaithful Judah*." Somehow I hear someone from the "not my people Ephraim-Israel" crowd shouting out: "Hey, that's not fair!" Indeed, said the clay to the Potter. Yes, idolatry leads to division and both have their consequences—envy, strife, jealousy, divorce, hatred and on and on.

Just to be clear, Judah's status (not divorced) had everything to do with the "sure mercies of David" (Isa. 55:3; Acts 13:34) and Moses' prophetic utterance: "*The scepter shall not depart from Judah, nor the staff from between his feet, until Shiloh comes and the allegiance of the nations is his* [and that Shiloh is the Lion of the Tribe of Judah]" (Gen. 49:10).

Could I gander that Judah's harassment of Ephraim via her isolation by Ephraim has caused Judah provocation? What I mean is this: We from among the nations brought into the Commonwealth of Israel view our "sister" with jaundice eye. Sorry, it's the truth of the matter. It is one thing to provoke to "righteous jealousy" but quite another simply to provoke them by getting them angry at us by our behaviors of the past—examples abound (edicts, ghettos, inquisitions, pogroms, the Holocaust, forced conversions, ad nausea, ad infinitude). I'm not saying the door swings one way—the "feeling is mutual" and the Bible says so—but there arises today the "*Repairers of the Breach*" (Isa. 58:12) to counter these ancient jealousies and strife!

Notwithstanding all this divine orchestration due to man's sinfulness and unrighteous behavior: the "Breach of Jeroboam" is healed by His stripes! And those who "stand in the gap" attest: No longer shall Judah harass Ephraim nor Ephraim simply provoke Judah.

But I purposefully digress—let's examine how we have purposefully or inadvertently "ghettoized the Jew" in our theological efforts at isolation . . .

> The problem is that those who do not see this unity between the two (the Church and Israel) assign the Church a position on the outside, leaving the Jews, national Israel, in a confined place, thus keeping the Jews theologically ghettoized, creating a false dichotomy.

To explain this erroneous theological concept, I have to resort to what I'm very familiar with and provide a visual aid to help you understand what I mean by a theological ghetto created for the Jews. By this I mean to bring to your attention the topography of the Jewish ghetto of Venice (Italy) which offers the perfect visual aid for considering the actual state of theology of some people in the Church.

As Italian, I know Venice well. For this reason, whenever I have the opportunity, I like bringing people to Venice and tour them around, and in a special way, I like to take them to the Jewish ghetto with the goal of offering them the best possible visual aid thereby teaching them a practical lesson. One year, I had the grace of organizing a week-long Christian board-meeting for a group of brothers coming from all over the world, right there, in the heart of the Jewish ghetto. It was an unforgettable experience, to say the least.

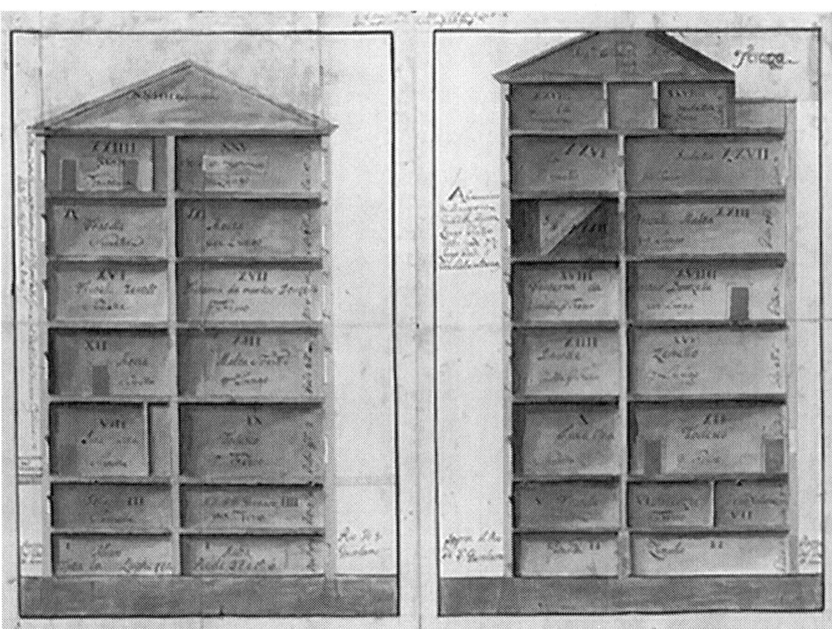

Figure 1 - Rendering of a vertical section of a building in the Ghetto Nuovo by Giorgio Fossati, 1777, typical of the oldest structures in the Ghetto, with shops at the lowest level and residences above.

Visiting Venice involves frequently shifting one's eyes between wondrous beauty and maddening crowds of tourists. The city's old Jewish ghetto, set back from the main attractions, has neither the hordes—though more and more people do stop by—nor the spectacular architecture of other neighborhoods. But as tourists walk across the old and new Jewish ghetto of Venice, you can pause and reflect on a relevant message transpiring from its very layout.

Figure 2 - Jewish Ghetto in Venice, Italy

For example, you would consider the high buildings that were constructed so that more people could be concentrated as to form what then became a ghetto, understood as a closed city district in which the Jews were segregated.

By the way, the original term was a Venetian dialect word coined in 14th Century Venice, whose name *getto* means to cast and to merge metals because of an old coppery foundry present in that area. The ghetto's enclosure was to be completed with two high walls: all exits were to be closed and the doors and windows that faced onto the external part of the ghetto were to be walled in and **custodians were assigned the task of surveying the gates both day and night.** As if that weren't enough, the Jews had to pay for two boats that were constantly travelled up and down the canals in the surrounding area. Any Jew found outside the ghetto at nighttime faced a very heavy punishment: a fine for the first and second offences, a heavier fine and two months imprisonment for the third.

In 1516 the Venetian Doge Leonardo Loredan issued a decree that recited:

> "All Jews are to live together in the courtyard houses that are found in the ghetto within the parish of San Gerolamo; and to prevent that they do not roam around at night, at the edge of the ghetto Vecchio and the ghetto novo two small access bridges will be utilized to be found on either side of these locations, that will be fitted with gates that will be opened in the morning and locked at midnight. **Four Christian custodians, who are to be government deputies and paid by same Jews at a price fixed by us, will watch these gates.**"[81]

It also established that they had to wear an identification sign and obliged them to manage pawnshops at rates established by the Serenissima, as well as to submit to many other onerous rules like

[81] https://en.wikipedia.org/wiki/Leonardo_Loredan

the prohibition of roaming Venice after nightfall. Consequently, this gave birth to the term that has since become synonymous with segregation and discrimination, pogroms and antisemitism.

The Venice Ghetto was one of the first-ever attempts to isolate Jews as that small island in the outskirts of the city, surrounded by canals and only three access points was ideal for this purpose. It was the beginning of the Jews being ghettoized. Similarities abound around the word regarding places of confinement, but the Venice Ghetto surpasses them all. You see, history tells us that Christians were delegated to the patrolling of the gates so that none of the Jews could exit by night with the task of keeping the Jews locked up inside the ghetto.

What a shame. This is akin to what happens today, when, despite the fact that the Lord has through His cross taken down this wall of partition, yet many are the believers who act as if were still in place, erecting a wall of separation—and theologically dressed it up in the form of "separate but equal"—American education knows what I mean by this.

Keeping the Jews in a theological ghetto equals to taking them into custody outside their own Commonwealth of Israel *de facto* ghettoizing them. Maintaining a strict separation between Israel and the Church has always produced a belief system that sees the Church inhabiting the spiritual benefits of the household of God as the true Israel of God. Frankly speaking, this is shortsighted spirituality, to say the least. This is precisely what I want to convey to anyone I bring to the Jewish ghetto of Venice—that through a practical and visual aid (the canals that surround it and make it an island within an island, the seclusion, the high walls) people may understand that in the minds and theology of many, the existence of a wall of partition (separation) is still erected there!

The truth is exactly the opposite, and echoing Doug Krieger's masterful presentation on this topic, I concur that "The blood of the Cross liberates the Jews from their theological ghetto."[82] Amen! Let's pronounce that they've been liberated from this ghetto by way of the Cross! Distinction YES – Separation NO! After all, Yeshua "***came and preached peace*** *to you who were off and* ***to those who were near***" (Eph. 2:17). Several excerpts from Krieger's tome will elaborate upon the theological ghettoization of the Jew:

> "The Blood of the Cross can only produce One New Man—so making peace! The cross does not sequester the Jews, National Israel, as defined by the Dispensationalists, to a "this worldly" destination *outside* the One Body, while the Bride of Messiah is assigned to an "other worldly" location. No, the Blood of the Cross liberates the Jews from their theological ghetto via the "divine deliverance" recorded in Romans 11:26; to wit: *"Blindness in part happened to Israel until the fullness of the Gentiles* [lit. "the multitude of nations"] *has come in . . . and so ALL ISRAEL will be delivered, as it is written, 'The Deliverer will come out of Zion, and He will turn*

[82] Douglas Krieger, *Commonwealth Theology ... An Introduction*, p. 172 (Tribnet Publications, 2018)

away ungodliness from Jacob; for this is My covenant with them, when I take away their sins' (Romans 11:25-27).

"ALL ISRAEL bespeaks of those from the "*multitude of nations*" as well as Judah's portion in Israel! BOTH HOUSES of Israel—Judah and Ephraim—ALL ISRAEL experiences the marvelous salvation of the Messiah-Deliverer Who shall '*come out of Zion*!'

"In sum: The cross cannot produce any other outcome (there is no 'tribulational interruption')—the biblical narrative is simply and overwhelmingly in counter distinction to Miles J. Stanford's[83] two gospels, two new covenants, two salvations, two "spheres" or administrative jurisdictions (viz. the New Jerusalem in the heavens *not* descending to the earth at the commencement of the Millennial rule and reign of the Son of David and the Holy District seen by Ezekiel in Ezekiel 40-48) or two Holy Cities, two brides (viz. the Wife of Jehovah and the Bride of Messiah/Jesus, the Christ). The Blood of the Cross has but ONE DETERMINATION that is a teleological reality: The Bride of Messiah—our God is NOT a polygamist (if I could be so crude)."[84]

By according the Jew some sort of "prophetic fulfillment status" in the sweet by-and-by as if this separating designation is somehow contained within God's Eternal Purpose is antithetical to

---

[83] The works of Miles J. Stanford can be view at this site: https://www.milesjstanford.com/ Retrieved on 03.15.2023.

[84] Douglas Krieger, Ibid, pp. 172-173

His immediate and unified goal. Moreover, they who exegete Galatians 6:16 wherein they lay emphasis upon a Greek conjunction (*kai* – KJV: *"And as many as walk according to this rule, peace be on them, and mercy* [exclusively this "peace and mercy" is upon the uncircumcised Gentile believer ***AND*** *upon the Israel of God"*–the claim is made that this ***AND*** separates out the Jews as the only Israel of God, while excluding the Gentile believer from the Israel of God]).

In ascribing "Peace and mercy" to the uncircumcised Gentile believers in the province of Galatia, and then the same to the Jews, as the "Israel of God" they have butchered the entire intent of Paul's writing to the Galatians! The NIV captures the essence of Paul's determination for both Jew (circumcised) and Gentile (uncircumcised) to live by the Truth of the Gospel (Gal. 2:5, 14) as His New Creation which alone avails (Gal. 6:15-16):

> *"Neither circumcision nor uncircumcision means anything; what counts is the new creation. Peace and mercy to all who follow* (lit. "walk in step as in a military march") *this rule* (standard) – *even to the Israel of God"* (Gal. 6:16) (or *"they are the Israel of God* " - Galatians 6:16 - GWT).

Therefore, let's join with Him in His liberation campaign that *"the word of the Lord may run swiftly and be glorified"* (II Thessalonians 3:1) proclaiming with boldness that God's great purpose for the Congregation of Israel was never for separation, but for unity. With this book I've been trying to demonstrate this truth believing that the work of restoration involves the view in

Commonwealth Theology which offers a much better expression of divine truth without diminishing Israel (Replacement Theology) or ghettoizing the Jew.[85]

[85] Douglas Krieger, Ibid, p. 197

Chapter 14

The Balance of Truth

More illumination from the Scriptures has come to us in these last years in favor of a balanced view which sees the whole community of Israel as an organic entity, through seeking the proper knowledge of its components, because God wants us to have a biblically based organic faith wherein a new paradigm that combines a theology which does not replace nor subsumes nor separates the Jewish people—yet makes scriptural sense in that the identity of the 'Church' in her relationship to the promised New Covenant is intrinsically linked with Israel (Judah and Ephraim).

In his groundbreaking book '***Commonwealth Theology … An Introduction***',[86] Doug Krieger believes that this new paradigm can offer to us the keys to interpret this holistic vision while meeting the expectations of any diligent student of the Bible. In other words, Krieger postulates that there is YES DISTINCTION between Israel and the Church because we see the Jewish people as the House of Jacob (aka Judah) which comprises both believing and unbelieving Jews wherein there is NO SEPARATION, because of their mutual

---

[86] Douglas William Krieger, *Commonwealth Theology, An Introduction* (Tribnet Publications 2018)

citizenship in the Commonwealth of Israel. Additionally, unlike any other position, Commonwealth of Israel Theology affirms that there is ***no separation*** from Judah (or the House of Jacob, the Jews, the broken off branches, those gathered in Eretz Israel in unbelief) and the House of Joseph, Ephraim (the Christians).

Preparatory to the fundamental understanding of this balanced view within Commonwealth Theology, the reader will have to recognize that for centuries the Church (aka, His Ekklesia) has been busy only with herself to the exclusion of the physical progeny of Abraham; thus, completely dismissing the Jewish element of her faith: are not we nurtured from Jewish soil after all? Even though the Church was born out of the Jewish people.

This "Jewish soil" provided the internationalization of the gospel going to the nations in fulfillment of the promise made to Abraham. Notwithstanding, Judah is given short shrift . . . hardly contemplated by the Church as an integral part of the divine equation because their "institutional framework" brought too much baggage with it and all sorts of frustration (viz. Judaizers who tried to get Gentile believers to be circumcised for salvation—Acts 15:1: "*Certain people came down from Judea to Antioch and were teaching the believers: 'Unless you are circumcised, according to the custom taught by Moses, you cannot be saved.'*"). So, "let's throw the baby out with the bath water"—which the Church summarily did; whereupon

Emperor Constantine outlawed all Jewish holidays as anti-Christian practices and customs in 329 AD:

> ". . . it appeared an unworthy thing that in the celebration of this most holy feast we should follow the practice of the Jews, who have impiously defiled their hands with enormous sin, and are, therefore, deservedly afflicted with blindness of soul . . . Let us then have nothing in common with the detestable Jewish crowd; for we have received from our Saviour a different way."[87]

These ancient and altogether atrocious edicts pronounced by Roman Emperor Constantine have beclouded the elect from among the nations from seeing their heritage with Judah (ours is a Hebraic heritage "*root that bore us*"—"*. . . do not consider yourself to be superior to those other branches* [Judah]. *If you do, consider this: You do not support the root, but the root supports you*" [Rom. 11:18].).

Judah (most ethnic Jews) have not yet seen His full deliverance of our common calling. Yes, we affirm Paul's understanding that in Christ there is neither "*Jew nor Greek, there is neither slave nor free, there is neither male nor female; for you are all one in Christ. And if you are Christ's, then you are Abraham's seed, and heirs*

---

[87] Eusebius, *Life of Constantine Vol. III Ch. XVIII Life of Constantine (Book III)* (Catholic Encyclopedia)

according to the promise" (Galatians 3:28-29); however, none of these juxtapositions eliminates the blatant fact that we still "are" *Jews, Greeks, slave, free, male or female*. What we from among the Gentiles have done is to assert our "Greek" status above that of our "Hebrew" origins!

The balanced view of Commonwealth Theology does a new thing, it looks at the future to the time when ***ALL ISRAEL*** will comprise both the multitude of nations as Ephraim—along with the "*rest of mankind*" (Acts 15:17) —and unbelieving ethnic Jews who will experience salvation in Messiah. It sets the record straight, demonstrating that the Ekklesia has a responsibility to regard the unity of her components—with the increase in the knowledge of God's purposes over which we now bear special responsibilities. In Commonwealth Theology you will finally see "ISRAEL" formed as THE STICK OF JUDAH (the Jewish people, both believing and

This clarifies that the identity within the Commonwealth of Israel (Eph. 2:12) comprises both believing and unbelieving Jews and the called out from among the nations, the Christians. In other words, as portrayed in the vision of the two sticks, we (the Stick of Joseph/Ephraim) have a prophetic destiny with the Jewish people (the Stick of Judah) and both of us constitute "***the whole House of Israel***" (Ezek. 37:11). (Please see paragraphs below expanding these statements.)

unbelieving) and THE STICK OF EPHRAIM (the elect from among the nations).

I would like to clarify what I mean in the highlighted block prior to this *paragraph* wherein I state: "This clarifies that the identity within the Commonwealth of Israel (Eph. 2:12) comprises both believing and unbelieving Jews and the called out from among the nations, the Christians."

This statement must be taken "prophetically" in that "unbelieving Jews" due to the prophecies of both Ezekiel 37 regarding the *Two Sticks* and Paul's statements in Romans 11:24 (". . . *who are natural branches, be grafted into* ***their own olive tree***") provide a "prophetic status" to Jews that is unique to this particular ethnic group.

"*In Christ*" there is "*neither Jew nor Greek*" (Gal. 3:28-29; Eph. 2:14); however, in the grand scheme of His Eternal Purpose the Almighty has predetermined (prophetically) to heal the "Breach of Jeroboam" and to bring together the 12 Tribes of Israel (Rev. 7:1-9; Ezek. 40-48) and to "*graft them in again*" wherein "*all Israel will be saved*" (Rom. 11:23, 26). Yes, this is an "ongoing process" from the cross forward until the prophetic consummation—viz. " . . . *the fullness of the Gentiles/Nations be come in*" (Rom. 11:25).

Therefore, Judah's (Jewish) participation is unambiguous in both the one Olive Tree and the Commonwealth of Israel—their association is "prophetically irrevocable" and awaits fulfillment as in ". . . *And so all Israel will be saved* (or "*delivered*"), *as it is written: 'The deliverer will come out of Zion, and He will turn away ungodliness from Jacob; for this is My covenant with them, when I take away their sins"* (Rom. 11:26-27; Psa. 14:7; Isa. 59:20-21).

It is in this sense Paul clearly states in Romans 11:28-32 the following:

> *"Concerning the gospel they are enemies for your sake, but concerning the election they are* ***beloved for the sake of the fathers. For the gifts and the calling of God are irrevocable.*** *For as you were once disobedient to God, yet have now obtained mercy through their disobedience, even so these also have now been disobedient, that* ***through the mercy shown you they also may obtain mercy.*** *For God has committed them all in disobedience, that He might have* ***mercy on all.****"*

I would hasten to add that "*committed* ***them*** *all in disobedience*" is all-inclusive of both Jews and Gentiles: ". . . *that He might have* ***mercy on all.***" Who is " . . . ***beloved for the sake of the fathers***"? To whom are "***the gifts and the calling of God . . . irrevocable***"?

To deny these are the "natural branches" or the "stick of Judah" (viz. the JEWS) flies in the face of prophetic fulfillment and is a shameful acquiescence to a "Triumphal Christianity" committed, if I can be utterly frank, to annihilation of the Jews (historically and into the future). The plain meaning of both the prophets' and the apostles' writings suffers corruption when those who distort the Scriptures delight in opposing the Almighty's inexorable prophetic quest in which: "*Ephraim's jealousy will cease, and Judah's harassment will be eliminated. Ephraim won't be jealous of Judah, and Judah won't harass Ephraim*" (Isaiah 11:13 – Common English Bible). By "Judah" I specifically draw attention to the Jews and by "Ephraim" to the nations who are coming into the Commonwealth of Israel as the "wild branches" of the one Olive Tree (Jer. 11:16).

Likewise, you will see the amplification of the "*Ekklesia in the Wilderness*" (Acts 7:38)—which was clearly forecasted by virtually all the prophets to expand into the Ekklesia which Jesus would build—"*My Father's house shall be a house of prayer for all peoples*" (Matt. 21:13; Isa. 56:7; Jer. 7:11; Psalm 93:5). Indeed, Stephen's identification of the "*Ekklesia in the Wilderness*" was in "miniature" of the ultimate "Ekklesia" Jesus had in view—and, for that matter, far and beyond the "democratic assembly" of the Greeks . . . both models, however, laid stress upon "His Household" once restricted under the Old Covenant to Moses-Aaron, the Law . . . but now expanded in the

New Covenant through Jesus whereupon we read: "*The Law was given through Moses but grace and truth came through Jesus Christ*" (John 1:17 – NKJV).

In other words, the "Ekklesia" Jesus would build was far and away more participatory/contributory and certainly more inclusive than either the Aaronic Priesthood model displayed in the "wilderness" and certainly far more "democratic" than the secular model of the Greek assembly (See 1 Cor. 11:17-14:40)—but displayed "characteristics" of both models . . . awaiting the manifestation of "the city of the living God" viewed from "Mount Zion" and known as the "heavenly Jerusalem" or "*ekklesia of the firstborn*" - Hebrews 12:22-24:

> *"But you have come to Mount Zion and the city of the living God, the heavenly Jerusalem, to an innumerable company of angels, to the general assembly and* ***ekklesia of the firstborn*** *who are registered in heaven, to God the Judge of all, to the spirits of just men made perfect, to Jesus the Mediator of the New Covenant, and to the blood of sprinkling that speaks better things than that of Abel."*

This paradigm enters the theological arena thereby amending the endless distortions and doctrinal inaccuracies, as well as theological misconceptions which have so long attempted to disinherit both Jews and Christians (see footnote on pp. 33-34) excluding one another from their common inheritance in the Commonwealth of Israel. The result of this "mutuality" is that the tenets of Commonwealth Theology provide evidence whereupon the reconciliation of Judah and Ephraim, the repairing of the breach, is *de facto* coming to its epiphany.

How do we know that? Well, if you are careful enough to observe the signs of the times you certainly can concur and conclude we are living in the days of prophetic regathering—the final revival/harvest. *"Son of man, can these bones live?"* (Ezek. 37:3) YES, together they most definitely shall arise a mighty army before the Lord as the breath of the Spirit of God is breathed into them! Listen up—perhaps you thought that "just the Jews" will arise a mighty army in the last days? Well, think again, and read again: *"Then He said to me: 'Son of man,* ***these bones are the whole House of Israel****'"* (Ezek. 37:11 – NKJV). It is abundantly clear that by saying "*the whole House of Israel*" in context with Ezekiel 37:15-28 the Almighty has in view the House of Judah and the House of Ephraim wherein they are prophetically designated to be *"One Stick in the Hand of the Lord"* (Ezek. 37:19) or, again, as it states in Ezekiel 37:11: *"The whole House of Israel."*

As the Jewish people are regathered from the four corners of the world to the Land of Israel, we are witnessing another ingathering taking place—the prophecy of the reunification of the Two Sticks, where both Houses (Judah and Ephraim) are being called home into the "***Household of God***" (Ephesians 2:19) with each part bearing a prophetic role to fulfill.

Thus, our inclusion into the Commonwealth of Israel brings to our attention the ongoing fulfillment of the prophecy of the Two Sticks (Ezek. 37:15-28) being reunited while at the same time repeatedly emphasizing these two components stand as distinct but not separated in the economy of God.

Personally, I have been many years engaged in supporting the reunion of the natural branches of the Olive Tree (the ethnic Jews - the Stick of Judah) to their own Land of Israel in fulfillment of a regathering in unbelief (Ezekiel 36) in view of their ultimate salvation; I had been a strong advocate of Commonwealth Theology even without knowing it—and convinced, today, many of you reading this for the first time are now being confirmed in your understanding of the same! The practice of anticipating and embracing our prophetic destiny with Judah, looking at the time of our unity in Messiah (when "*All Israel shall be saved*" – Rom. 11:26) gives tremendous credibility to the developing of a theology that centers around this final consummation. Prior to this fulfillment, Israel and the Church currently have a prophetic role to play awaiting their most glorious hour when they will be summoned by God to prophesy together during the final drama of history known as Daniel's Seventieth Week. I strongly believe that coming to appreciate our identity in this Messianic Community (The

Commonwealth of Israel) will make our quest consummate; consequently, a much fuller understanding of the phrases found in Revelation 14:12: "*Here is the endurance of the saints who keep the* ***commandments of God*** *and* ***the faith of Jesus***." It's pretty difficult to assume, as some denominations do, that those keeping the commandments of God are somehow exclusively Christians—especially since Revelation 7 provides us the unification of the 12 Tribes of Israel (Rev. 7:1-8 – those who "*keep the commandments of God*") juxtaposed to that great multitude "*from every nation, tribe, people and language, standing before the throne and before the Lamb*" (Rev. 7:9-17 – "*and the faith of Jesus*"). Yes, there's definitely overlap here; however, it's difficult to close your eyes to the distinctions represented here culminating in the overwhelming unification found in Revelation 7: "*the great multitude . . . from EVERY NATION, TRIBE, people and language.*" (Note: Last heard Israel constituted themselves as a nation, and very tribal; a people with their own language.)

I believe that this steady and well-adjusted approach is one of the greatest advancements in our understanding of the purpose of God in this, perhaps, the latest decade as it really represents a well-balanced view, a wondrous prophetic statement in that unbelieving Jews/National Israel shall one day come into full prophetic fulfillment at the end of days. This is to say that prophetic Judah (Jacob, National Israel) is already with us in the Commonwealth of

Israel because even in their current unbelief they have a most peculiar prophetic destiny for which Almighty God is gathering them back into the Land of promise.

In other words, we do anticipate, in faith, their grafting in again into the one common root which bears both the natural and wild branches (*"For God is able to graft them in again . . . the natural branches, be grafted into their own olive tree!"* – Rom. 11:23-24).

Understanding our collocation[88] in the Family of God has become quintessential to our enjoyment of the blessing of being in the *national life of Israel* (Eph. 2:12 CJB) because the goodness of the Lord is not only that He cleanses us of our sins—forgetting the past—but that He has lifted us up to a place of honor calling us His people, sharing with us the promises originally belonging only to Israel; only to the House of Judah—for the House of Israel was given a ***"certificate of divorce"*** (Jeremiah 3:8). We have not replaced Israel

---

[88] Collocations are partly or fully fixed expressions that become established through repeated context-dependent use. Such terms as 'crystal clear', 'middle management', 'nuclear family', and 'cosmetic surgery' are examples of collocated pairs of words. Collocations can be in a syntactic relation (such as verb-object: 'make' and 'decision'), lexical relation (such as autonomy), or they can be in no linguistically defined relation. Knowledge of collocations is vital for the competent use of a language: a grammatically correct sentence will stand out as awkward if collational preferences are violated. This makes collational an interesting area for language teaching. (Source: Wikipedia, Retrieved on 08.05.2020)

in the plan of God, we only have been awakened to our original but renewed wedding covenant (Rom. 7:1-4)—we have become a new corporeity and citizenship that finds its fulfillment in the soil of Hebraic roots. I know for certain that it is not done unintentionally.

Simply put, the Commonwealth of Israel (Jews and Gentiles meeting and sharing the same status in the Household of God) is out of the equation, perhaps because this was not yet the time for the Body of Messiah to apprehend this positional truth? One thing is most certain, many Jews were temporarily broken off from the Olive Tree of Salvation—from the common Root that is the source of Life (Romans 11:13-24), allowing us from among the nations—"elect from among the nations"—to be grafted into the same One and only Olive Tree (Jeremiah 11:16).

The breaking off of the natural branches vs. the grafting in of the wild branches must be understood in the context of Jeremiah 11:16, where it says "*The LORD called your name, Green Olive Tree*." So, there is only one "***Green Olive Tree***"—which bespeaks the same thing corporeity and citizenship "organically expressed." Furthermore, and again in context, this "*Green Olive Tree*" alludes to "*Both Israel and Judah*" (Jer. 11:10) – two branches, ultimately, of the same *Green Olive Tree*.

The grafting in of the wild branches substantiates the Commonwealth of Israel, the spiritual citizenship of all Israel. Our inclusion or collocation brings us near the universal assembly of the saints (from both Old Testament and New Testament) through the mediator of the New Covenant. Therefore, the image of the TWO having become ONE, the ONE NEW MAN, and the ONE BODY is a way to explain the multi-diversity of the Ekklesia. From whatever side, you arrive at the same expression, view. It follows that having come close to the Household of God, it allows us to widen our circle, enlarge the stakes of our tent and refocuses our vision.

Gentiles who have come to faith in the God of the Hebrew Scriptures (i.e., the "*Prophetic Scriptures*"—Romans 16:26) have been grafted into God's family Tree of Salvation and covenant relationship—together with the Jewish people we have become fellow citizens in the Commonwealth of God's eternal Israel . . . we are no longer aliens. We are now naturalized citizens of this Commonwealth.

We are Abraham's children and heirs according to the promises made by God to Abraham. Christian Scriptures permit believers in Yeshua to join the Jewish people and the Nation of Israel as part of the greater Household of God, sharing both the blessings and the responsibilities of biblical faith so that now, they—those having been shown mercy—have the greater responsibility for establishing the means of coming alongside the Jewish community in true fraternal relationship because the "elect from among the nations" have been the greater source of division through its overt persecution of the Jewish people for the past two millennia (e.g. "Constantinian Christianity" with edicts separating the "Christian House from the Jewish House").

On the next two pages you will find a summary of Commonwealth of Israel Theology compiled by Dr. Douglas Hamp who serves on the Board of Directors of the Commonwealth of Israel Foundation . . . a board upon which I also serve. I felt Dr. Hamp's concise presentation of the core affirmations of Commonwealth Theology would be extremely helpful as a sort of panoramic view of CT.

COMMONWEALTH OF ISRAEL THEOLOGY SUMMARY

God elected Israel (Deut. 7:6) and entered into a marriage contract with her at Mt. Sinai (Exo. 24:7-8, Jer. 31:32), commonly referred to as the Old Covenant. Sadly, instead of being faithful, Israel repeatedly went after other gods (Jer. 3) which lead to the split of the united kingdom into the southern kingdom of Judah (house of Judah under Rehoboam) and the northern kingdom of Israel (House of Israel/Ephraim under Jeroboam) (1 Kings 11:31-32). Finally, after seven hundred years of adultery since Sinai, God gave the northern kingdom a certificate of divorce and sent her away (Jer. 3:8, Hos. 2:2), calling her No-Mercy (*Lo-Ruhamah*) and Not-My-People (*Lo-Ammi*) (Hos. 1:8-9) and she (ten tribes) assimilated into the pagan gentiles (nations) (Hos. 7:8, 8:8, 9:17, 2 Kings 17:23-24). Judah likewise deserved divorce but God would not because of his promise to David (Hos. 1:7, 1 Kings 11:32).

God then promised to betroth the house of Israel to himself in righteousness (Hos. 2:19) and to restore the two kingdoms into one (two sticks per Ezek. 37:16-23). That promise created a divine dilemma because God's instructions (law) did not permit a woman to come back to her first husband after she had been married to others (Deut. 24:1-4) (that was the curse of the law) (Gal. 3:13). This divine dilemma was resolved by Jesus' (the husband's) death which canceled the Old (Marriage) Covenant

Now those who were not his people (Rom. 9:24-26) and who had not obtained mercy (1 Pet. 2:10) could come into the commonwealth of Israel as full members and citizens (Eph. 2:11-19) which was also in fulfillment of Ephraim becoming the multitude of nations (Gen. 48:19, Rom. 11:25).

Commonwealth of Israel Theology Elevator Pitch

Commonwealth of Israel Theology teaches that God married Israel at Sinai (Old Covenant). Israel was unfaithful, divided into two kingdoms, and then God divorced the northern kingdom (though Judah deserved it too). He then promised to betroth Israel again but the curse of the law (due to adultery) prevented that. Only through the death of the husband, Jesus, could the curse be removed and could Israel (scattered and assimilated into the nations) come back to God. The good news is they/we can be full members of the Commonwealth of Israel and God will restore the two houses into one.

Commonwealth of Israel Theology Tagline

COI Theology teaches the good news that we gentiles can be full members of the Commonwealth of Israel and that Israel and Judah will be restored into one nation.

Summaries compiled by Dr. Douglas Hamp

Chapter 15
Called to Family Reunion

With respect to the relationship between that multinational company known as the Commonwealth of Israel, and God's eternal purpose, the entire theological argumentation used by Paul addressing the Ephesians has to do with the Gentiles becoming fellow citizens . . . who in Christ are no longer aliens but part of the same body with those of the stock of the House of Judah (the Jews)—thus becoming one body.

As elucidated throughout this book, the whole community of Israel, is therefore the living Corpus of Messiah and, according to the biblical logic followed by this writer, becomes Israel (in a broader sense – whose Hebrew meaning connotes: "God Contended" – "Wrestles with God" – "Triumphant with God" or "A Prince with God").

Paul well-said "*There is one body*" (Ephesians 4:4). If we now read what Paul intends by "*then all Israel shall be saved*" in Romans 11:26, then it makes sense, and the right perspective opens up to clarify that the Commonwealth of Israel is not a post-Cross reality, but that **all Israel** is comprised of BOTH "*the multitude of the nations*" (Romans 11:25) as Ephraim and unbelieving Jews of Judah who experience National Deliverance via the Deliverer/Messiah Who "*will come out of Zion*" (Romans 11:25-27).

It should also be considered that even the sages in Israel say that the expression *all Israel* has a broader meaning. In fact, it is a recurring expression in Jewish literature, where it need not mean "every Jew without a single exception," but "Israel as a whole." Thus, "all Israel has a portion in the age to come," says the Mishnah tractate Sanhedrin (10.1), and proceeds immediately to name certain Israelites who have no portion therein.[89]

Perhaps we should change our paradigm on the way we have seen the "All Israel" up till now?[90] Unless we understand Torah and the way Paul taught with his rabbinical background, we will never be able to connect the mysteries Paul is trying to bring forth from the prophetic Scriptures. In Ephesians 3, when the apostle talks about mystery, he is going into Torah teaching while explaining it. There are things that in Christ the people of old could not comprehend (such as the new birth as the greatest miracle of all). So,

---

[89] Bruce, F.F., *Romans: An Introduction and Commentary* (InterVarsity press, 1985), p. 218

[90] There is a great book by Chad J. Schafer and Doug Krieger which delves into this aspect of ALL ISRAEL. It pretty much has to do with the two houses of Israel—Judah and Ephraim. The book is called *The World in the Bondage of Egypt . . . Under the Triumphal Arch of Titus* (Tribnet Publications 2016)

what is this mystery? Simply put, "*that the Gentiles should be fellow heirs of the same body*" (Ephesians 3:6).

It becomes more complicated when you consider that in all Systematic Theology you are presented with two distinct bodies, two houses (Israel and the Church kept separated), when in Christ Jesus there is only One Body. Just because someone is a Jew does not mean that he is part of that One Body of the redeemed (if not for those who will be grafted in their natural olive tree). This is the Remnant grafted into the One Olive Tree and that is why God relates us to Israel, "*to make all see what is the fellowship of the mystery*" (Ephesians 3:9).

This is altogether essential. So, what is my connection in that mystery? Once again, the New Testament provides ample proof of this reality. I remember years ago the Holy Spirit enlightened me expanding this concept while reading John 11:52. In this instance, the High Priest, Caiaphas, prophesied with John, the Beloved, extending his prophecy beyond the immediate:

> *"'You know nothing at all, nor do you consider that it is expedient for us that one man should die for the people, and not that the whole nation should perish.' Now this he did not say on his own authority; but being high priest that year he prophesied that Jesus would die for the nation,* ***and not for that nation only, but also***

> ***that He would gather together in ONE the children of God who were scattered abroad***" (John 11:49-52).

When I saw this, I exclaimed: "It is right there in plain sight; how could I have not seen it before, we are ONE?" Yet, there are many today who when they read John 11:52 "*Not for that nation only, but also that He would gather together in one the children of God who were scattered abroad*" either consider those scattered abroad are only Jews, since they conjecture that all Jews constitute all Twelve Tribes or generic believers in Messiah from all the nations (including the Jews) who have received the New Covenant given to the Church as a result of the Kingdom's rejection by the leadership of the Jews at the time of Jesus' earthly ministry. However, what John said in these passages (John 11:47-53) is utterly profound.

Let me repeat, John said that "*Now this he* (Caiaphas) *did not say on his own authority; but being high priest that year he prophesied that Jesus would die for the nation*" (i.e., for Judah) . . . then John doubles down and declares: "*And not for that nation only, but also that* ***He would gather together in one the children of God who were scattered abroad.***" What could John have meant by this additional statement? The 'nation' in the eyes of Caiaphas simply meant the Jews of Judea, but John amplified it adding an additional component, to include not only the Jews of Judea but all Twelve Tribes scattered abroad as did James, the half-brother of Jesus in James 1:1, "*James, a bondservant of God and of the Lord Jesus Christ, To* *the twelve tribes which are scattered abroad.*" The recognition of these so-called "lost tribes" (i.e., Ephraim, the Ten-Northern Tribes of Israel deported, scattered among the nations) ***"He would gather together in one the children of God who were scattered abroad."*** We simply cannot isolate these prophetic statements made by John from those rehearsed by Paul in his epistle to the Romans when Paul quoted from Hosea regarding the Gentile inclusion into the Household of Faith, to wit:

> "*. . . and that He might make known the riches of His glory on the vessels of mercy, which He had prepared beforehand for glory, even us whom He called,* **NOT OF THE JEWS ONLY, BUT ALSO OF THE GENTILES?** *As He says also in Hosea: 'I will call them My people, who were not My people, and her beloved, who was not beloved.' 'And it shall come to pass in the place where it was said to them, 'you are not My people,' there they shall be called sons of the living God'*" (Romans 9:23-26).

And, this, Paul said in direct reference to Israel-Ephraim who had been divorced and were no longer His people! When I received revelation from the Holy Spirit in Romans 9:24 I immediately saw another glaring evidence that ***"Even us whom He called, not of the Jews only*** (The House of Jacob/Judah), ***but also of the Gentiles"*** (The House of Ephraim, those who were swallowed up of the nations). Those whom He called are none other but the Ekklesia that Yeshua is building in the here and now, the assembly of the called out (comprised of both Jews and Gentiles)—the gathering of the Lord. And again, just after this incredible statement Paul goes on describing the Gentiles/Nations by quoting directly from Hosea:

> *"I will call them My people, who were not My people, and her beloved, who was not beloved. And it shall come to pass in the place where it was said to them, 'You are not My people,' there they shall be called sons of the living God"* (Romans 9:25-26).

In this context it is important to have a glimpse of God's prophetic declaration recorded in Hosea to add another piece to the puzzle. Hosea begat three children through the harlot, Gomer. The first was **Jezreel**, meaning *God sows*; the second was named **Lo-Ruhamah** meaning *not loved/no mercy*. The third was named **Lo-ammi** meaning *not my people*. These names were used to refer to Israel . . . where it says:

> *"So he went and took Gomer the daughter of Diblaim and she conceived and bore him a son. Then the LORD said to him, 'Call his name Jezreel' . . . And she conceived again and bore a daughter. Then God said to him: 'Call her name Lo-Ruhamah, For I will no longer have mercy on the house of Israel, But I will utterly take them away. Yet I will have mercy on the house of Judah, Will save them by the Lord their God, And will not save them by bow, Nor by sword or battle, By horses or horsemen.' Now when she had weaned Lo-Ruhamah, she conceived and bore a*

son. Then God said: 'Call his name Lo-Ammi, For you are not My people, And I will not be your God'" (Hosea 1:2-9).

Immediately following the names of these three children, God brings up all three names and declares:

> *"Yet the Israelites will be like the sand on the seashore, which cannot be measured or counted. In the place where it was said to them, 'You are not my people,' they will be called 'children of the living God.'* ***The people of Judah and the people of Israel will come together;*** *they will appoint one leader and will come up out of the land, for great will be the day of* ***Jezreel*** [God sows]. *'Say of your brothers, 'My people'* [ammi] *and of your sisters, 'My loved one* [ruhamah]' (Hosea 1:10-2:1).

These are the same terms that are found in Hosea 2:23:

> ***"Then I will sow her for Myself in the earth,*** *And I will have mercy on her who had not obtained mercy; Then I will say to those who were not My people, 'You are My people!' And they shall say, 'You are my God!'"* (Hosea 2:23).

As Jamie Perez condenses, ". . . in the valley of Jezreel, where God once sowed Israel's destruction and disowned her, God will sow forgiveness and re-unite her with the house of Judah."[91] This is

[91] Jamie L. Perez M.Ed, *ibid*, pp. 201-202

simply a remarkable summary of the whole purpose of God for the reuniting of His people, not for their own innate goodness or value, but for His own glory.

So, coming back to Caiaphas' statement in John 11 regarding that Jesus would die for the nation, it is not coincidence that immediately afterwards Jesus left Bethania to go "*into the country near the wilderness, to a city called **Ephraim**, and there remained with His disciples*" (John 11:54). Ephraim means *two fold increase* or *fruitful.*

There's a connection here, don't you think? In other words, Paul directly identifies Ephraim's presence within the context of the Gentiles/Nations wherein they were assimilated, swallowed up. But it is in the New Covenant's elucidations in both Jeremiah and in Ezekiel described as "*an everlasting covenant with them*" (Ezek. 37:26) which we see the two becoming as one.

This "*covenant of peace*" mentioned in Ezekiel, is in point of fact, the very NEW COVENANT—so making peace then and there. Yes, Ephesians 2:15—for there is but one New Covenant of Peace!

> "*. . . that He might reconcile them both to God in ONE BODY through the cross, thereby putting to death the enmity*". . . "*to*

create in Himself ***one new man*** *from the two, thus making* ***peace***" (Eph. 2:15-16).

First, the New Covenant promise was exclusively made "*with the HOUSE OF ISRAEL and WITH THE HOUSE OF JUDAH*" (the two houses) which are then addressed in Jeremiah 31:33:

"*But this is the covenant that I will make with* ***THE HOUSE OF ISRAEL*** *after those days, says the LORD: I will put My law in their minds, and write it on their hearts; and I will be their God, and they shall be My people.*"

> Here we can see the two houses as ONE and only ONE House of Israel.

As per the New Covenant I do not see different Covenants as dispensationalists affirm keeping apart Israel and the Church thus creating a dichotomy. Nor do I see as some in this theological system that today's New Testament saints experience only the "spiritual blessings" of the New Covenant promised in the Old Testament, but not the New Covenant *per se.*

Indeed, John Nelson Darby taught that the Ekklesia of our Lord Jesus simply enjoys the spiritual blessings of the New Covenant but not the New Covenant promised—it was exclusively promised to Israel (as per his understanding of who constituted Israel). The list of those who keep the Jews ghettoized is exceedingly long.[92]

Suffice it to say that disassociating Ephraim from the Nations/Gentiles is theologically incorrect, for they were assimilated and lost among the nations but now through the blood of His Cross

> They are citizens of the national life of Israel and are, therefore, no longer aliens. Moreover, the original promise of the New Covenant (Jeremiah 31:31-36; Ezekiel 36:26-27) and its spiritual blessings were and still are committed to both Houses of Israel (the whole Twelve Tribes of Israel), and even more in that Ephraim's dispersion among the nations was God's ultimate intention of expressing the entry of the Gentiles into the Commonwealth of Israel. This is the greatest expression of the call

those who "*were **afar off** have been **brought near***" (Eph. 2:13) and are no longer strangers but are considered members of the household of faith!

---

[92] For a comprehensive and extended treatise on the erroneous theological system that keeps Israel and the Church separate or replaced, please read the groundbreaking work of Douglas Krieger, *Commonwealth Theology – An Introduction*, Tribnet Publications, 2018 @ https://www.amazon.com/Commonwealth-Theology-Douglas-W-Krieger/dp/1977951643/ref=tmm_pap_swatch_0?_encoding=UTF8&qid=1592055967&sr=8-7

I have also come to apprehend that the mystery is solved in the words of Jesus in John 10:16 where he says, "*And other sheep I have which are not of this fold; them also I must bring, and they will hear My voice; and there will be* ***ONE FLOCK*** *and one shepherd.*"

Like in the days of Jesus, He is still operating among His children as He wants people to open their eyes that they might see the reality of the one flock. One day He said, "*You do not believe because you are not of MY SHEEP*" (John 10:26). Jesus talks about one flock and ONE sheepfold. To me it is perfectly clear.

Expressed in another way, the call to family reunion is but a shadow of the UNITY we are called to keep in the Body of Christ. Jesus prayed for unity of all believers down to our present day:

> "*I do not pray for these alone, but also for those who will believe in Me through their word; that they all may be ONE, as You, Father, are in Me, and I in You; that they also may be ONE in Us, that the world may believe that You sent Me. And the glory which You gave Me I have given them, that they may be one just as We are one: I in them, and You in Me;* ***that they may be made perfect in ONE****, and that the world may know that You have sent Me, and have loved them as You have loved Me*" (John 17:20-23).

"*That the world may know*"—on this earth, in the here and now, not in the sweet by-and-by. When this UNITY of which Jesus earnestly prayed for will be reached here on earth, then the Ekklesia will be given herself to a prevailing witness to principalities and powers in the heavenly places of the manifold wisdom of God. She will be ready to meet her Bridegroom whereupon it will be as Jesus said, "*Many will come from east and west, from the north and the south, and sit down with Abraham, Isaac and Jacob in the kingdom of heaven*" (Matt. 8:11; Luke 13:29).

The best is yet to come!
Yes, it will be happen:

"They shall no longer be two nations, nor shall they ever be divided into two kingdoms again."

(Ezekiel 37:22)

Chapter 16
The Whole Community of Israel

Trying to ascertain who constitutes **the whole community of Israel** (all Israel) has been the aim of this book through the lens of God's eternal purpose.

As stated at the end of chapter 13, *all Israel* bespeaks of those from the "*multitude of nations*" (viz. Hebrew: "*Melo Hagoyim*"—Gen. 17:4-5; Strong's H1995, H1471)[93] as well as

---

[93] Initially, the Almighty promised that He would make of Abram a Great Nation (Gen. 12:3a) and that "in you all the families of the earth shall be blessed" (Gen. 12:3b)—that promise was repeated again in Genesis 15:5: "'*Look now toward heaven, and count the stars if you are able to number them.' And He said to him, 'So shall your descendants be.'*" The phrase "*multitude of nations*" is first used in Genesis 17:4-5: "*As for Me, behold, My covenant is with you, and you shall be a father of a multitude of nations. No longer shall your name be called Abram, but your name shall be Abraham; for I have made you a father of a multitude of nations.*" Likewise to Abraham's wife, Sarai, her name was changed as well to "*Sarah shall be her name . . . and I will bless her and also give you a son by her; then I will bless her, and she shall be a mother of nations, kings of peoples shall be from her*" (Gen. 17:15-16). This promise was extended through Isaac (Gen. 26:2-5); to Jacob (Gen. 28:3); to Joseph (Gen. 48:3-4); and thence to Ephraim (Gen. 48:13-20) ... Ref. Rom. 11:25; Isa. 8:14. The "son of promise" was in Isaac and clarified as "*the Seed*" (capital "S") to mean "*in Christ*" – "*Brethren, I speak in the manner of men: Though it is only a man's covenant, yet if it is confirmed, no one annuls or adds to it. Now to Abraham and his Seed were the promises made. He does not say, 'And to seeds,' as of many, but as of one, 'And to your Seed,' who is Christ. And this I say, that the law, which was four-hundred and thirty years later, cannot annul the covenant that was confirmed before God in Christ . . . what purpose then does the law serve? It was added because of transgressions, till the Seed should come to whom the promise was made; and it was*

Judah's portion in Israel and beyond! Both houses of Israel—Judah and Ephraim— *all Israel* experiences the marvelous salvation of the Messiah-Deliverer Who shall *'come out of Zion!'* (Romans 11:26-27) What I've tried to say in my exposition is that Jews and Gentiles (aka the elect from among the nations—Ephraim so scattered, swallowed up, assimilated) are not separated in the ultimate plan and purposes of the ages; they are distinct, yes, but not separated for they are attached to the same root and enjoy the same covenant in fullness at the coming of the Son of Man in glory.

The superfluous charge that we who affirm our identity with the Seed of Promise to be those "scattered" and/or "swallowed up" among the nations to be His "overflow" or "doubly fruitful" (which is the precise meaning of *Ephraim*) . . . "*who were not a people but now are the people of God* . . . (for) *"I will call them My people, who were not My people, and her beloved, who*

---

appointed through angels by the hand of a mediator." Isaac was offered up upon the altar, not Abraham; Isaac was the archetype of the Seed, which is Christ who was offered up for us all and in Christ, the Seed: "*But the Scripture has confined all under sin, that the promise by faith in Jesus Christ might be given to those who believe . . . For you are all sons of God through faith in Christ Jesus . . . For as many of you as were baptized into Christ have put on Christ. There is neither Jew nor Greek . . . if you are Christ's, then you are Abraham's seed, and heirs according to the promise*" (excerpts from Galatians 3).

was not beloved" . . . "And it shall come to pass in the place where it was said to them 'You are not My people,' There they shall be called sons of the living God" (Rom. 9:24-26; Hos. 2:23)—such a charge of identification with Israel by believers in Yeshua from among the nations is without merit. We are NOT replacing Judah—we are through Messiah utterly joined to them under the Tabernacle of David—his United Kingdom. We supplement Judah; not dispense with Judah!

In this light, *all Israel* is *the Israel of God in God's Eternal Purpose*. Here in full display it is the company of believers that live by the truth of the gospel, since God's new creation is what avails, for "*Neither circumcision nor uncircumcision means anything; what counts is the new creation. Peace and mercy to all who follow* (lit. "walk in step as in a military march") *this rule* (standard) – *even to **the Israel of God**"* (Gal. 6:16 NIV), or, "for *they are the **Israel of God** "* - Galatians 6:16 - GWT). Be it clearly understood, the conjunction found in sundry manuscripts and some English translations (i.e., "*And as many as walk according to this rule, peace and mercy be upon them AND upon the Israel of God*"—vs. 16) constitutes an horrific exegetical distortion when interpreted in this manner: designating believers from Gentile backgrounds (i.e., believers in Galatia) with "*peace and mercy be upon them*" AND then singling out believers from Jewish backgrounds as the singular, actual "*Israel of God*" completely misses the mark of the entire epistle to the Galatians. This eisogesis utterly distorts by designating the "*Israel of God*" as Jewish believers who enjoy the New Creation separate and apart from the peace and mercy accorded to Gentile believers in Yeshua.

Paul's entire effort in Galatians is abundantly clear: "*For as many of you as were baptized into Christ have put on Christ. There is neither Jew nor Greek, there is neither slave nor free, there is neither male nor female; for you are all one in Christ Jesus. And if you are Christ's then you are Abraham's seed, and heirs according to the promise*" (Gal. 3:27-29). The "*Israel of God*" is the crescendo of Paul's entire thesis. Indeed, if "*neither circumcision nor uncircumcision avails* (i.e., "neither Jew nor Greek") *but a New Creation*," then how is it that only Jewish believers are considered the Israel of God and Galatian believers from the "nations" are somehow left out of the Israel of God? Isn't "*the Israel of God*" the "*New Creation*" where there is "*neither Jew nor Greek*?" Listen up—there is neither male nor female but there are still "brothers and sisters"—likewise, there is neither Jew nor Greek but there are Jewish believers and those called out from the nations (aka, Gentile) believers-TOGETHER they constitute the Israel of God and upon them ***both*** abides His "peace and mercy!"

Beyond everything, the nexus of the mystery of the gospel can be summed up like this: ***"This mystery is that through the gospel the Gentiles are heirs together with Israel, members together of one body, and share together in the promise in Christ Jesus"*** (Ephesians 3:6 NIV).

Moreover, I would hasten to add that it is through the atoning sacrifice on the cross that a way was opened for reconciliation between the two. In fact, with Jesus' very death, according to Ephesians 2:17, "*He came and preached peace to you who were far away and peace to those who were near.*" A similar expression is found in a prophetic statement when Caiaphas prophesied that "*Jesus would die for the Jewish nation, and not only for that nation but also for the scattered children of God,* ***to bring them together and make them one***" (John 11:52 NIV).

Hence, I've tried to present the plan for ultimate reconciliation of *the whole community of Israel* by showing the ample evidence found in the Hebrew and apostolic Scriptures (Old and New Testaments).

The prayer of Daniel the prophet is just one marvelous example of God's very eternal purpose for the whole community of Israel, when he cried: "*Lord, you are righteous, but this day we are covered with shame—the people of Judah and the inhabitants of Jerusalem and* ***all Israel, both near and far****, in all the countries where you have scattered us because of our unfaithfulness to you"* (Daniel 9:7 NIV).

Furthermore, in chapter 14 I've stressed the fact that a balanced view is needed when it comes to define who's who in the citizenship *(politeia) of Israel,* in that the practice of anticipating and embracing our prophetic destiny with Judah, looking at the time of our unity in Messiah (when "*All Israel shall be saved*" – Rom. 11:26) makes us prophetically engaged. Unbelieving Jews/National Israel shall one day come into full prophetic fulfillment at the end of days, thus ending the mystery surrounding it, viz. God's plan concerning Israel's future considering her election in the past and her present deviation - National Israel is a mystery primarily because her election is superimposed on the present hardening that has resulted in her "*blindness in part*" or "*partial blindness.*"

At this juncture I would like to highlight the obvious. The "*fullness of the Nations has come in*" (Rom. 11:25) is intrinsically connected with the immediate statement following: "*And so all Israel will be saved* (i.e., delivered), *as it is written: 'The Deliverer will come out of Zion, and He will turn away ungodliness from Jacob; for this is My covenant with them, when I take away their sins*" (Rom.

11:26-27). Again, to suggest that somehow the *"fullness of the Nations has come in"* (which statement alludes precisely to the expression of the *"Melo Hagoyim"* or *"multitude of nations"*) "escapes" from "Jacob's Trouble" is, in a word, preposterous! By interpreting deliverance from tribulation accords the *"fullness of the Nations be come in"* and then for the Jewish People (the "all Israel" in the eyes of "Christian escapists" or "separatists") to "face the music"(viz. Jacob's Trouble—Jeremiah 30:7) by himself without believers from the Nations is, again, a distortion of the plain meaning of the Scripture. What these "separatists" are suggesting is this: Those of the nations have already had their sins taken away through Christ—but those Jews have to undergo extreme tribulation (which we, already forgiven of our sins by the Deliverer, will not endure) in order for the Almighty to *"turn away ungodliness from Jacob."*

No, the *"fullness of the Gentiles be come in"* occurs **simultaneously** with the deliverance by the *"Deliverer"* on behalf of us BOTH (Nations and those of Judah) Who will *"come out of Zion."* It is He Who will deliver us both and at the close of the age with the completion of the very same promise found in Jeremiah 30:7: *"Alas! For that day is great, so that none is like it; and it is the time of Jacob's trouble, BUT HE SHALL BE SAVED OUT*

OF IT." And again: "*And at the time your people shall be delivered, everyone who is found written in the book*" (Dan. 12:1).

I say this not as some form of comfort to the Jewish people—that if we suffer, we suffer together—but more so because the very Word of God declares it! It is this insidious doctrine that the final purification of the "*holy people*" unilaterally refers to the Jewish people—Judah and has nothing to do with those from the nations who do not need to be delivered because they've been delivered already. "Let the Jews languish in their final 'trouble' while those called out from among the nations watch from their heavenly perches! Sorry, to express myself with such sarcasm; however, what all this distorted hermeneutic cries out is this: God has a plan for the Church and God has a plan for the Jews and never the twain shall meet—whereas it is the very Plan and Purpose of the Almighty in uniting His people together and to do so in a grand finale, crescendo at the close of the age! "*And so ALL ISRAEL shall be delivered*" and I might add: At the SAME TIME!

Therefore, our inclusion or collocation into the *one olive tree* automatically brings us near the universal assembly of the saints (from both Old Testament and New Testament) through the mediator of the New Covenant. Consequently, the image of the TWO having become ONE, the ONE NEW MAN, and the

ONE BODY is a way to explain the multi-diversity of the Commonwealth of Israel. From whatever side you look at it, you arrive at the same expression or view. It follows that having become members of the *Household of God (Ephesians 2:19)*, it allows us to widen our circle, enlarge the stakes of our tent and refocuses our vision.

Thus, the grafting in of the wild olive branch substantiates the whole community of Israel, the spiritual citizenship of **all Israel**, whereas it is a glaring fact that the Scriptures speak of a remnant that God always reserves for Himself. "*For they are not **all Israel** who are of Israel*" (Romans 9:6). As Jamie L. Perez points out, 'Israel's status with God is not determined by the sheer number of those who call themselves Israelites, but by those amongst the Israelites who are genuinely faithful to him'[94]. Paul seems to be indicating that a new entity is being formed within Israel, not outside of it or apart from it, but within it. This entity is the **Israel of God or Israel's "spiritual Commonwealth"**[95], composed of all those who placed their confidence in Messiah—Israel's suffering servant and Israel's coming King.

---

[94] Jamie L. Perez, ibid, p. 186

[95] Jamie L. Perez, ibid, p. 203

But this is not all since there is more than our inclusion into Israel's spiritual citizenship. In fact, I believe that we can't interpret the whole community of Israel apart from understanding our mutual experience in the gathering, without making reference to the Exodus vs Greater Exodus motive that runs through the Bible as a linear thread. To this end, it seems appropriate here to mention that in my first book, *Called to a Holy Pilgrimage*,[96] I've dealt extensively with the Exodus motive in salvation which provides a pattern for our spiritual Exodus, a type through which we identify our personal experience, foreshadowing a more fulfillment later of the same through a Greater Exodus to come. Here I'd like to quote from chapter 7 entitled "*The Adumbrative Language in Prophecy*":

"From this we understand that the Greater Exodus is comprised of both events leading up to the final regathering of the Jewish people to the land of Israel and the implications of this in-gathering to those called out from among the Gentiles –"*Now brethren, concerning the coming of our Lord Jesus Christ and our gathering together to Him*"— (2 Thessalonians 2.1). This is too incredible to comprehend to its fullest, but I do believe as the prophetic clock keeps ticking, the Holy Spirit will shed light into

[96] Gian Luca Morotti, *Called to a Holy Pilgrimage – The Gathering and Salvation of the House of Jacob*. The Adumbrative Language in Prophecy, chapter 7 (Commonwealth of Israel Foundation 2020)

this wonderful subject of the final and Greater Exodus. I hasten to add that the final Exodus is a type of the divine harvest at the end of the age described in Isaiah 27:12-13, to wit:

> *And it shall come to pass in that day that the Lord will thresh, from the channel of the River to the Brook of Egypt;* ***And you will be gathered one by one, O you children of Israel.*** *So it shall be in that day:* ***The great trumpet will be blown;*** *They will come, who are about to perish in the land of Assyria, and they who are* ***outcasts*** *in the land of Egypt, and shall worship the LORD in the holy mount at Jerusalem.*

This is the plucking up and gathering of all of the Lord's people, the conclusive ingathering, the time when **all Israel** (meaning all the children of Israel – both Houses – that of Judah and that of Ephraim) **shall be saved**—for when the "*fullness of the Nations has come in, THEN ALL ISRAEL shall be delivered*" (Romans 11:25-26); at the sound of the last great trumpet. As it states in Romans 9:6: "*But it is not that the word of God has taken no effect . . . for they are not all Israel who are of Israel, nor are they all children because they are the seed of Abraham; but 'In Isaac your seed shall be called.'*"

Now we understand why we can't interpret Romans 11:26 without the bedrock of Romans 9:6.

Finally, I would be remiss if I didn't conclude without mentioning the subject of the "*woman*" in Revelation 12, which to my view completes the picture of who is the whole community of Israel and wraps it all up.

> "***Now a great sign appeared in heaven: a woman clothed with the sun, with the moon under her feet, and on her head a garland of twelve stars.*** *Then being with child, she cried out in labor and in pain to give birth*" (Revelation 12:1-2).

This is not intended to be a comprehensive explanation but essentially, she represents that spiritual Israel that is more than Israel. It goes backwards through the line of the seed to Eve and forward to through the line of the seed to Mary and the Lord Jesus. The number twelve signifies completeness through divine government (3 * 4 = 12 – Triune God with Creation = Administrative Completeness [cf. Revelation 4:9; Revelation 7:4-8]), and as being the number of the tribes of Israel, which are the type of the spiritual Israel of God. The 144,000 found in Revelation 7 signifies the Divine Unity of His Holy People—truly the Israel of God. The unity of these 12 Tribes is immediately linked to the "*great multitude that no man could number . . . who have come out of the great tribulation and have washed their robes and made them white in the blood of the Lamb*" (Rev. 7:9-17). These in

Revelation of the 12 United Tribes are "*sealed upon the earth*" and those in Revelation 14:1-5 are the 144,000 standing with the Lamb on Mount Zion with the Father's Name on their foreheads having been redeemed from the earth. Heaven and earth united and ultimately the "12 Gates" of the New Jerusalem reflect the names of the 12 tribes of Israel (Rev. 21:12-13) and her "12 Foundations" those of the 12 Apostles of the Lamb (Rev. 21:14); i.e., 12 * 12 = 144. Indeed, the 12,000 furlongs ("*length, breadth, and height are equal*"—Rev. 21:16) continuously amalgamate the unity of the 12 Tribes and the 12 Apostles in that 12,000 * 12,000 = 144,000,000 sq. furlongs and all six of its faces (as a cube)—yes, distinct, but inseparable but all united as the Groom's Bride (Rev. 21:9-11).

There are a plethora of commentaries and acclaimed Bible studies by scholars who see the woman of Revelation 12 as the entire community of Israel, of God's faithful people waiting for the coming of Messiah[97]. The woman is therefore the entire

---

[97] *Grant R. Osborne, Revelation (Baker Academic 202), p. 456-457*
'She represents the whole people of God, Israel and the church. The 12 stars probably represent the whole people of God. While the woman may be married in 12-5, even there she symbolizes the whole people of God.'

Barnhouse, Donald, Grey, Revelation...An Expositional Commentary, Zondervan, Grand Rapids, MI, 1971, p. 216 (quoted in 'The Two Witnesses Vol. II – Douglas W. Krieger, Tribnet Publications 2014)

community of Israel, then the one new man of Ephesians 2, the congregation of true believers in Yeshua, both Jew and Gentile.

I've got the sense that I've just scratched the surface here, but we are beginning to see that there is more than we thought there was, that our story is intertwined with that of national Israel, the Jews, the tribe of Judah, the regathered exiles to their Land from the four corners of the world.

Reader, in that the "*Deliverer will come out of Zion*" (Rom. 11:26) then it follows—and this is NOT a quantum leap nor conjecture—that anti-Zionism is against the One Who comes out of Zion!

> *"Why do the nations rage, and the people plot a vain thing? The kings of the earth set themselves, and the rulers take counsel*

'The woman, the, represents not merely Israel 'of whom concerning the flesh, Christ came' (Rom. 9:5), but is that spiritual body of elect from the very beginning of the history of man, by whom God had eternally purposed to bring naught the revolt of Satan'.

Cambridge Bible for Schools and Colleges: *"More certain is the reference, or at least similarity of imagery, to Genesis 37:9, where "the eleven stars," i.e. signs of the zodiac, represent Jacob's eleven sons, bowing down to Joseph, the twelfth. Here, the ideal Israel appears in the glory of all the patriarchs: Abraham, Isaac and Jacob, and their wives, are hers, and of the Twelve Tribes none is wanting. The whole description, in fact, is interpreted in Romans 9:5."*

https://biblehub.com/commentaries/revelation/12.htm

together, against the LORD and against His Anointed (i. e, His Messiah or Deliverer), saying, 'Let us break Their bonds in pieces and cast away Their cords from us.' He who sits in the heavens shall laugh; the Lord shall hold them in derision. Then He shall speak to them in His wrath, and distress them in His deep displeasure: 'Yet I have set My King on My holy hill of Zion'" (Psalm 2:1-6).

From beginning to end the Exodus of the children of Israel mirrors our salvation; and we are grateful to the Lord, for our destinies meet in the Greater Exodus at the end of this present age. My prayer is that we'll keep asking God to show us more of His plan that we can meditate on His wonderful works and that we may come to appreciate all that we share with the royal house of Judah—so much so that He has promised that He shall take the "Stick of Ephraim and the stick of Judah and make them ONE stick" in His hand—that sounds like "One Olive Tree" and it is!

Finally, let us be fully assured, the all-inclusive New Jerusalem is comprised of both Houses as the true and only Israel of God whose gates bear the names of the Twelve Tribes of Israel and whose foundations the Twelve Apostles of the Lamb—because the Deliverer has surely come out of Zion to deliver All Israel . . . this most assuredly is His ultimate Ekklesia for:

> "*. . . you have come to Mount Zion and to the city of the living God, the heavenly Jerusalem, to an innumerable company of angels, to the general assembly*[98] *and church* (lit. "*Ekklesia*") *of the firstborn who are registered in heaven, to God the Judge of all, to the spirits of just men made perfect, to Jesus the Mediator of the New Covenant, and to the blood of sprinkling that speaks better things than that of Abel.*" (Hebrews 12:22-24)

Deeply ponder the Good Shepherd's words: *"I lay down My life for the sheep . . . and other sheep I have which are not of this fold; them also I must bring, and they will hear My voice; and THERE WILL BE ONE FLOCK AND ONE SHEPHERD"* (John 10:15b-16).

Amen.

[98] (Strong's: G3831 (fig.) universal companionship . . . The ***pangeguris*** refers to that solemn assembly gathered for festal rejoicing used in Heb. 12:23 to represent the church (Ekklesia) in heaven whose earthly toil and suffering has forever passed away [cf. Rev. 21:4])

Appendix
Definition of Terms

The proper use of words perhaps is the most tactic weapon at our disposition if we want to see our prayers hitting the mark on behalf of the truth. As in information warfare it is very important that the transmitter be consistent, or the message might be misread. It follows that the use of words is very critical. That's why, by consent of the COIF[99] I wanted to include as Appendix of my book an extract from the groundbreaking work called 'Commonwealth Theology Essentials' to offer the reader a unique opportunity to examine and dissect all the terms used to identify Israel and the Church, by providing solid ground to learn how to disambiguate the most common terminologies used to refer to God's chosen people. The following is taken from the Introduction of the book.

---

[99]This author sits on the BoD of the Commonwealth of Israel Foundation (COIF), a non-profit organization whose aim is to follow Paul's example in teaching the good news that we gentiles can be full members of the Commonwealth of Israel and that Israel and Judah will be restored into one nation. In 2020 the Foundation published a groundbreaking book called ***Commonwealth Theology Essentials***, written by Douglas Krieger, Douglas Hamp, Gavin Finley, and Chris Steinle. Please visit the website at https://www.commonwealthofisrael.org/p/resources.html, and here https://www.amazon.com/dp/B088X3ZJBR. The content of this appendix Reproduced with the Permission of the Commonwealth Of Israel Foundation.

The bottom line is that a re-examination of mainline Christendom's position on the relationship between Israel and the Church, the very terms, "Israel" and "Church," is needed, therefore cannot remain ambiguous. When it comes to this particular theological field of Israelology—especially, whoever controls the meaning of these words, controls the theological position regarding Israel: past, present, and future. Although we are intensely focused, at the same time, the "theological ramifications" are all encompassing - impacting every branch of theology. Some words (terms) used in the Bible are actually ambiguous - even in their original language. Most unfortunately, what is meant by the words "Jews" and "Israel,"—in the Bible and in modern culture - must either be defined by the context in which the words are used or by purposefully adding further clarification. This is grievously problematic in any theological analysis of these two entities; and yes, "Jews" and "Israel" are quite often two separate entities when used in the Bible.

Complicating the issue is the fact that the contemporary usage of these words often refers to a different entity than the same word represented when the Bible was written. Or, the same word might define a related entity of different composition than its historical equivalent. This "time shift" of usage can be observed even between Old and New Testament writers. Now compound all of these moving pieces with the honest efforts of modern Bible translators, who have tried to represent the identity of these ancient entities by stating them in modern terms - terms which carry current connotations based on current usage.

Furthermore, missing the true, or at least the best, definition of these terms might occur innocently or because of intentional bias. We will not, at this time, attempt to attach blame except to note that Early Church theology developed in a social and political climate in which the Jews were detested. The important thing to know for now is that Commonwealth Theology takes great care to determine what is meant when references to Israel, et. al. occurs in the Bible. The rest of this section will examine how these terms can be used. Just becoming aware of the variety of definitions is a step toward identifying the correct meaning of these words when reading the Bible; and of course, when formulating theology.

DEFINING JEWS, ISRAEL, AND THE HOUSE OF ISRAEL

WHO ARE THE JEWS?

Jews: ambiguous: Israel: related to any tribe, Modern Israel.

Jewish ethnicity, nationhood, and religion are strongly interrelated, as Judaism is the ethnic religion of the Jewish people, while its observance varies from strict observance to complete nonobservance. [https://en.wikipedia.org/wiki/Jews] "A person born Jewish who refutes Judaism may continue to assert a Jewish identity, and if he or she does not convert to another religion, even religious Jews will recognize the person as a Jew." [Ernest Krausz; Gitta Tulea. Jewish

Survival: The Identity Problem at the Close of the Twentieth Century; [... International Workshop at Bar-Ilan University on the 18th and 19th of March, 1997] [Transaction Publishers. pp. 90–. ISBN 978-1-4128-2689-1.]

Jews: disambiguous: Judah; the **House of Judah**.

The Greek term was a loan from Aramaic *Y'hūdāi*, corresponding to Hebrew יְהוּדִי *Yehudi*, originally the term for a member of the tribe of Judah or the people of the kingdom of Judah. According to the Hebrew Bible, the name of both the tribe and kingdom derive from Judah, the fourth son of Jacob. ["Jew", Oxford English Dictionary.]

The English word "Jew" continues Middle English Gyw, *Iewe*. These terms derive from Old French *giu*, earlier *juieu*, which through elision had dropped the letter "d" from the Medieval Latin *Iudaeus*, which, like the New Testament Greek term *Ioudaios*, meant both "Jew" and "Judean"/ "of Judea" [*Encyclopedia of the Peoples of Africa and the Middle East*, Facts On File Inc., Infobase Publishing, 2009, p. 336].

SPEAKING OF ISRAEL

Israel: ambiguous: All Israel; the United Kingdom. According to Wictionary; 1. "The State of Israel, a modern country in the Middle East, at the eastern shore of the Mediterranean. 2. The Land of Israel, a region that is roughly coextensive with the State of Israel. 3. (historical) An ancient kingdom that occupied roughly the same area in ancient times. 4. (historical) An ancient kingdom that occupied the northern part of this area, as distinct from Judah. 5. The Jews, taken collectively." [https://en.wiktionary.org/wiki/Israel]

Israel: disambiguous: Referring to the northern 10 tribes of the divided kingdom; the **House of Israel**, also known as Ephraim, Samaria, the Stick of Joseph, Jezreel; which were taken into captivity cir. 745-712 BC by the Assyrians and were assimilated among the nations. These Israelites constitute those nations identified in the blessing given to Abraham, Isaac and Jacob and conferred upon Joseph's younger son, Ephraim, where he would become a "*multitude of nations.*" [CT,p10]

When the word "Israel" is used in the Old Testament what is it referring to? That depends on where in the saga of the Children of Israel the word appears. Obviously, before Jacob's descendants settled in the Land - and before the northern and southern settlements came to odds - "Israel," as a nation, continued to denote the "Children of Israel" as a whole. However, once this North-South faction developed, the definition of "Israel" began to change.

THE HOUSE OF ISRAEL AND THE HOUSE OF JUDAH

The following text takes place just prior to the union of the northern and southern tribes.

2 Samuel 2:8: *But Abner the son of Ner, commander of Saul's army, took Ishbosheth the son of Saul and brought him over to Mahanaim;*

> *9 and he made him king over Gilead, over the Ashurites, over Jezreel, over Ephraim, over Benjamin, and over all Israel. 10 Ishbosheth, Saul's son, was forty years old when he began to reign over Israel, and he reigned two years. Only the house of Judah followed David. 11 And the time that David was king in Hebron over the house of Judah was seven years and six months.*

In the passage above, the United Kingdom under David had not yet been formed. The southern tribes (with Benjamin), gathered under Saul, are here referred to as "Israel;" and even "all Israel," along with the ten northern tribes – collectively, these twelve tribes are referred to as "Israel."

Notwithstanding the fact that Judah was aligned with King David. Judah was not considered to be part of "all Israel" in this case because "all Israel," as well as the nomenclature, "Israel," represented what would, after the Breach of Jeroboam, be designated "*the House of Israel*." Note that the tribe of **Judah** is, however, called out as the **House of Judah.**

From this point on - in the Old Testament - "**Israel**" often referred to the **northern territories** of the Promised Land. As of the passage above, these two would-be kingdoms had already been ruled by two separate kings.

Example:

In 1 Kings 1:35, King David had just declared Solomon to be king. The Kingdom had not yet been "formally" divided. The verse, nonetheless, reads: *"For I have appointed him to be ruler over Israel and Judah"*; signifying the **House of Israel** and the **House of Judah**.

The meaning of "Israel" and "Judah" MUST be established by the context of their usage. Often in the case of prophecy, the time and jurisdiction of the prophet must be discovered in order to establish a verse's correct context.

ISRAEL AND JEWS IN THE NEW TESTAMENT

When it comes to the New Testament - and especially when these terms appear within quotes from the Old Testament - the same process of discovery must be applied in order to disambiguate their meaning. Furthermore, the Old Testament meaning of references to "Israel," "Judah," and "Jews" within such quoted verses must be respected when interpreting the New Testament passage in which these words occur.

The history and prophetic significance of BOTH houses of Israel carried over into New Testament times. As formerly noted, Jesus made reference to the lost sheep of the House of Israel. Moreover, Peter's first sermon mentions and even indicates the location of the two houses at that the beginning of the first century. Perhaps because Judah had not been formally divorced by God as the House of Israel had been, Peter honored the order recorded by Paul as *"first to the Jew, then to the Greek."*

Peter began his Day of Pentecost sermon by addressing the House of Judah: "*Men of **Judah*** (*Ioudaioi*) *and all who dwell in Jerusalem*" (Acts 2:14). Recall that Daniel used this same wording to address "those near": "*To the men of Judah, to the inhabitants of Jerusalem* . . . ." Later in his sermon, Peter acknowledged those from among the nations, who had been specifically identified in verses 9-11, as those who had traveled from foreign lands for the feast: "*Therefore let all the **house of Israel** (oikos Israel, οἶκος Ἰσραὴλ) know assuredly that God has made this Jesus, whom you crucified, both Lord and Christ*" (Acts 2:39).

Index of Names

E

F

G

K

L

M

N

O

P

R

S

About the Author

Gian Luca Morotti sits in the Board of Directors of the Commonwealth of Israel Foundation (COIF), a non-profit organization whose aim is to follow Paul's example in teaching the good news that we gentiles can be full members of the Commonwealth of Israel and that Israel and Judah will be restored into one nation. He holds a degree in Security Management and a bachelor in Hebraic Heritage Studies. He currently serves as member of the International Board of Ebenezer Operation Exodus International, a ministry helping the Jewish People making Aliyah. He is the author of the book ***Called to a Holy Pilgrimage – The Gathering and Salvation of the House of Jacob.***

Commonwealth of Israel Foundation Books

(Click on image to review/purchase book)

THE UNTOLD STORY OF GRACE IN THE SECOND TEMPLE PERIOD

DR. DOUGLAS HAMP
CHRIS WINTERS STEINLE

THE
DENVER
DECLARATION

WITH BIBLE
REFERENCES

Commonwealth
Of Israel Foundation

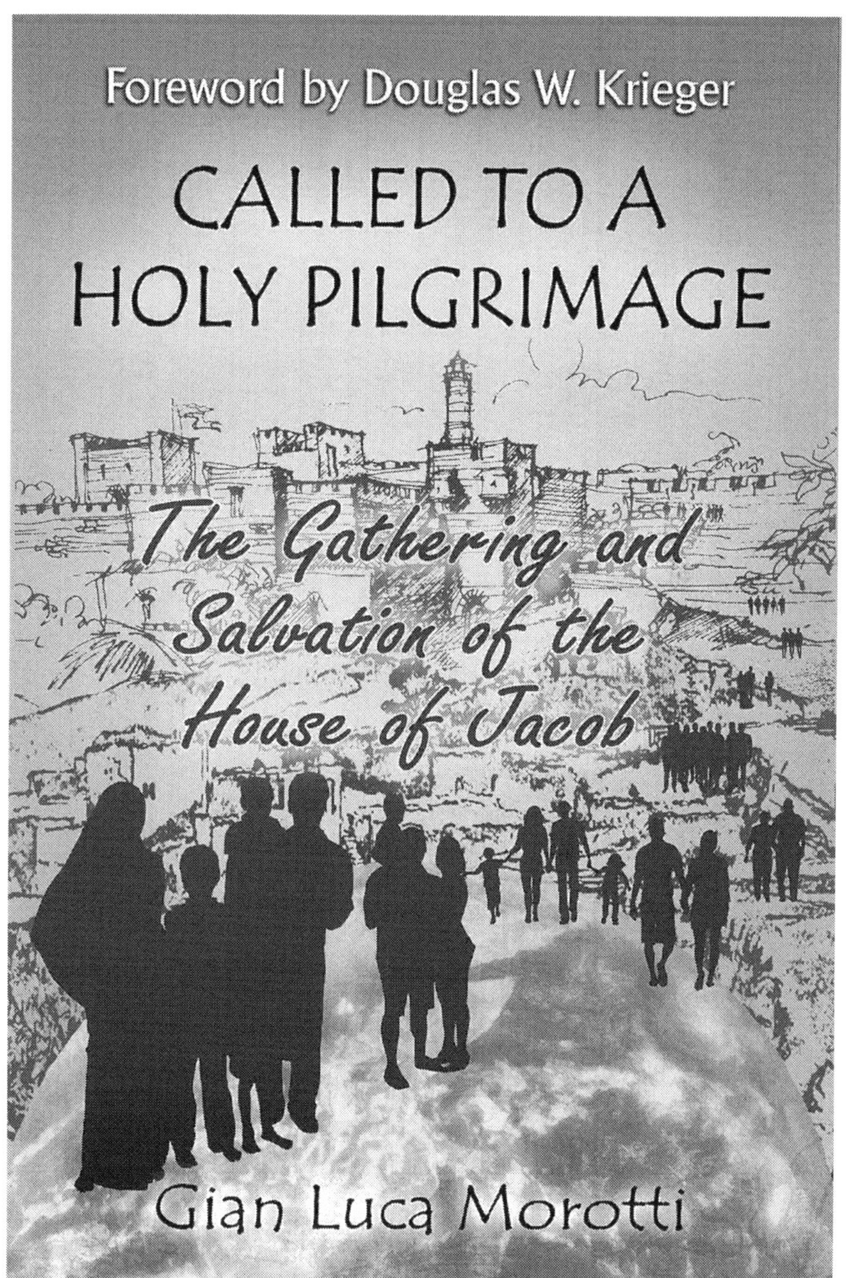
Foreword by Douglas W. Krieger
CALLED TO A
HOLY PILGRIMAGE
The Gathering and
Salvation of the
House of Jacob
Gian Luca Morotti

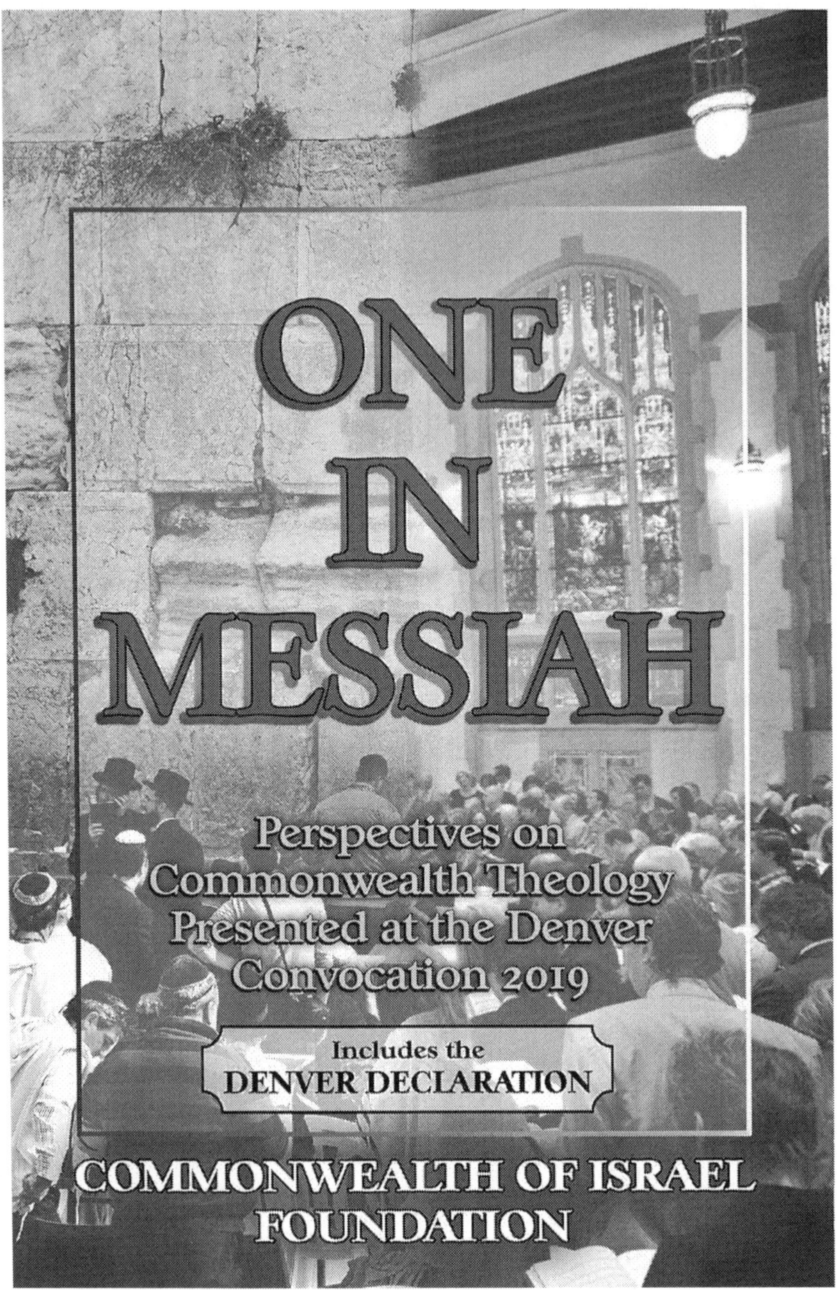
ONE
IN
MESSIAH
Perspectives on
Commonwealth Theology
Presented at the Denver
Convocation 2019
Includes the
DENVER DECLARATION
COMMONWEALTH OF ISRAEL
FOUNDATION

Made in the USA
Columbia, SC
27 June 2024

37526698R00136